C000268678

'Most precious stones form und
has let her own trials and suf
this thought-provoking and pra
reflections.'

*J.John, canonjjohn.com*

'The way we handle personal trials and suffering is an indicator
of our true character. For Emily Owen, her trials and challenges
have produced a woman of deep wisdom and godly character.
Emily's writings, prayers, and life lessons learned from men and
women in the Bible will guide you on your own journey and
ignite your faith in God's loving care for you.'

*Elizabeth George, author*

'This is a devotional with a difference. Each chapter focuses on
a different biblical character, and a different "calling card" that
God uses to remind us of his presence. Emily creates a beautiful tapestry with her words, effortlessly weaving imagined
thoughts from each character with her own stories as well as
other Scriptures on a similar theme. And the poetry she creates
captures precisely what each chapter is about. Almost 'stream
of consciousness' in places, her writing pours forth biblical
knowledge, as she moves from Old to New Testament and back
again, revealing the overarching themes of God's grace and love
throughout the Bible.'

*Claire Musters, writer, speaker and editor,*
*clairemusters.com*

'This book is full of poignant reminders that God is not satisfied with a distant, dutiful relationship, he died on the cross to bring us close to himself; to take away every barrier that would come between us and him. These thought-provoking readings will help us to be real, and to enter in to the joy of God's intimate presence.'

*Marilyn Baker,*
*singer/songwriter and Director of MBM Trust*

'I so loved this book. From page one I felt as if I'd stepped into a train and was being taken on a journey. It was an exciting journey because the end destination was unpredictable and the unfolding landscape was constantly changing. I found myself moved from laughter to tears; from heart searching challenge to deep comfort and reassurance; from holy inspiration to profound personal reflection.

'With great skill Emily steps from the viewpoint of various Bible characters into her own stories which she shares with wonderful realism and poignancy; then into a tapestry of beautiful scriptures, powerful reflections and searching prophetic responses from the Lord.

I don't hesitate to recommend *God's Calling Cards* to you.'
*Tracy Williamson, author and speaker with MBM Trust*

'Emily Owen's writing never fails to inspire. In this book, through her honesty, she helped me to strip away all pretences and draw close to the very heart of God, no matter the circumstance.'

*Wendy H. Jones,*
*author and President of the Scottish Association of Writers*

# GOD'S CALLING CARDS

## Personal reminders of his presence with us

*Emily Owen*

**Authentic**

First published 2019 by Authentic Media Limited,
PO Box 6326, Bletchley, Milton Keynes, MK1 9GG.
authenticmedia.co.uk

**British Library Cataloguing in Publication Data**
A catalogue record for this book is available from the British Library.
ISBN: 978-1-78893-025-3
978-1-78893-026-0 (e-book)

Cover design by Shelepa Mykola
Printed and bound by CPI Group (UK) Ltd., Croydon, CR0 4YY

# Contents

Introduction                                             1

1    Adam and Eve (Genesis 3)                            5
2    Hagar (Genesis 16; 21)                             23
3    Abraham (Genesis 22)                               41
4    Moses and the Burning Bush (Exodus 3; 4)           57
5    Moses Up the Mountain (Exodus 19)                  75
6    Moses and the Cloud (Exodus 24)                    91
7    Samuel (1 Samuel 3)                               109
8    Israel (Hosea 11)                                 125
9    Ananias (Acts 9)                                  135
10   God (Jeremiah 33)                                 157
11   Paul (Philippians 3)                              173

     Final Bit                                         191
     Acknowledgements                                  197
     Notes                                             198

For Abigail, Josiah, Caleb, Micah and Elianne

Thank you for bringing me a lot of joy.
Thank you for being in my books:
I hope you don't mind in years to come!
Thank you for giggles and questions and stories and fun.
Thank you for sometimes not quite knowing if I'm
'one of the adults' or 'one of you'.
Without you, I wouldn't be Aunty Memem.

# Introduction

I know I might be about to state the obvious, but being deaf means that I can't hear. I can't hear when people call to get my attention.

My nephew, ever since he was about 3, has taken it upon himself to be an 'Aunty Memem Educator'. In other words, he tells people how they can get my attention.

'You need to go near her, and tap her on the arm if she doesn't see you, then when she is looking at you, you can talk to her, but make sure she can see your lips or she won't know what you are saying.'

That's the gist of it, anyway, and Caleb is right. For people to call me, they need to come close.

So, to me, calling has become synonymous with being close to someone. And not only physically. In a way, receiving a text, or an email (or a phone call), is someone calling. Someone saying, 'In this moment, I am close to you.'

When we call, often it's because we'd like someone's attention. More than that, we'd like their presence with us.

'I am close to you.'

In this book, we'll look at times in the Bible when God, or an angel of God, called to someone.

He wanted their attention. And, into their situations, he came close.

Close enough to call.

The first record of God calling is in Genesis 3, when he calls to Adam: 'Where are you?'
We'll look at that in more detail in chapter 1.
Adam was hiding but God came close enough to call.
**Where are you? I want to know.**
And that desire from God to know where we are echoes on and on.
Calling to us.
**Where are you? Tell me.**
But, like Adam, sometimes we are afraid of where we are.
Or we don't like it.
Or we don't want to be there.
We hide.
And God calls.
Even in our not wanting to be seen, he calls.
He gets our attention.
He asks for our presence.

Let's make sure we are looking.

> *I lift up my eyes to the mountains – where does my help come from? My help comes from the LORD, the Maker of heaven and earth.*
>
> Psalm 121:1,2

Adam, in his hiding, made clothes for himself. And God, in his grace, said, 'you can have better than that.' Even in Adam's fear, God gave him different clothes. Grace-clothes. We, too, can wear different clothes. So often, we make do with things we provide for ourselves. God says 'you can have better than that' and he gives us

*a garment of praise instead of a spirit of despair.*

Isaiah 61:3

We'll look at examples of self-made clothes and God-made clothes in this book.
Grace-clothes.
Ways God reminds us of his presence with us.
His calling cards.

Calling cards are believed to have originated in China, during the sixteenth century, and soon spread until they were widely used across the world.[1]

Calling cards are personalized cards, which were left in homes to announce that someone had visited, so the home owner knew who had called. A sign that someone had been there. A sign that someone wanted to meet with, or get to know, or spend time with them.

God leaves calling cards. Personalized things which remind us of his presence.
Things which say **I've been here; I am here; I'd like to spend time with you**.

*But now, O Jacob, listen to the LORD who created you.*
*O Israel, the one who formed you says, 'Do not be afraid,*
*for I have ransomed you. I have called you by name; you*
*are mine.'*

Isaiah 43:1, NLT

Emily

# 1

# Adam and Eve
(Genesis 3)

 *But the* LORD *God called to the man, 'Where are you?'*

v. 9

My niece was 2 the first time she asked me to 'play hide seek'.
I said, 'OK, who hides first?'
A squealed 'Me, me, me!'
I said, 'Right, I'll stay here while you hide.'

I closed my eyes and loudly and slowly counted to ten. Preparing to noisily go from place to place, unsuccessfully looking for her, I opened my eyes. And I saw that 'not seeing her' would be harder than I'd thought. She was standing right where she'd been before I closed my eyes. The only difference was, she was now standing with her hands over her eyes.
She thought she was hiding.
'I can't see me, so I'm not here . . .'

I must admit, I probably wouldn't have called it a hippopotamus. But Adam really liked that name.

We have such a good life. Living in this beautiful garden, naming the animals, just enjoying every day. There's a snake that keeps hanging around, which is a bit of a nuisance, but I'm getting used to it popping up. I wasn't sure about it at first, but it's not doing any harm. Sometimes I even have a chat with it.

Yesterday, though, it was more than a chat. I was standing in the garden, near the tree of the knowledge of good and evil, when the snake appeared. Now, way back at the beginning, when God made Adam, and just before God made me, he said to Adam, 'Don't eat the fruit on that tree. Any other is fine, but not that one.' Adam told me that and he told me God said, if we eat that fruit, we will die.

I'm not sure what dying is, but it must not be a good thing? So I've never really thought about the tree. There's lots of other things to eat. But when the snake came up yesterday, it made me think about it.

'Did God really say, "You must not eat from any tree in the garden"?'[1]

Well no, God didn't say that. He only said we must not eat from that one tree. So I told the snake. And the snake almost laughed. It said 'You won't die if you eat from that tree!'

Looking back, I should have walked away right then. But there was something about the way the snake said it, almost as if it knew exactly the tone of voice to use to pique my curiosity.

'Your eyes will be opened and you'll be like God, knowing good and evil.'[2]

Knowledge is good, isn't it? I looked over at the tree as I thought about this. As I said, the tree has never really entered my thinking before, but now, because of the snake, I thought about it.

And then I looked at it. I was a bit surprised. Beautiful-looking fruit. How could anything that looks this good be bad for me?

I could feel the snake staring at me. I reached out, took some of the fruit, and ate it. I gave some to Adam, too, and he ate it.

The fruit was delicious. For about half a second.

As soon as I swallowed my first bite, maybe even sooner, I gained some knowledge alright. Not about the taste of the fruit – I can't even remember what it tasted like – but about embarrassment. I didn't know that's what it was called, that feeling that made me want to curl up and hide. I'd never felt it before. But now I was embarrassed, and all because I . . . well, I had no clothes on! I was naked. And so was Adam. We looked at each other. Then we tried desperately not to look at each other. Then we found some big leaves and sewed them together to cover us up a bit.

Bad though this thing called embarrassment was, it was nothing compared to the feeling I had when I heard God. He was walking in the garden. Usually, we can't wait to meet him and walk in the garden together. But this time, we went and hid behind a tree. It was as we were hiding, trying not to move, that we heard God's voice. Calling quietly but clearly: 'Where are you?' He'd never asked that before. He'd never needed to. We were terrified. We were scared to answer him. Scared to stop hiding. After all, we were naked! But then we realized there was something even more scary than answering him. Not answering him . . .

Adam and Eve have a good life. Except for one thing. The serpent.
But they ignore the serpent, and focus on all the good things God has given them.

Except they don't. The bad thing supersedes everything for them.

How often the same is true of us.

> *Since, then, you have been raised with Christ, set your hearts on things above, where Christ is, seated at the right hand of God. Set your minds on things above, not on earthly things. For you died, and your life is now hidden with Christ in God.*

> Colossians 3:1–3

Set your minds on things that are above . . . where Christ is.

Where is Christ?

Seated at the right hand of God, yes. But he is also the one who said, 'I am with you always.'[3]

Jesus Christ is right here. In the presence of God and in the presence of you.

Are you aware that he is in your presence?

Everywhere you go, Jesus is there, too.

If Eve had asked herself 'Where's God?' she'd have seen that God was all around. He hadn't gone anywhere.

She'd have seen, had she asked, 'Is God in this suggestion?' as she looked at the serpent, that God wasn't in it.

Life can be hard. Temptations come thick and fast.

And they are very real.

'Where's God in this?'

If he isn't, do you want to be?

'For you died, and your life is now hidden with Christ in God.'
Your life is encircled by Creator God himself. You don't
have to be swayed by suggestions he doesn't make, suggestions made by others apart from God.

Father God
Thank you for holding me.
Amen

Because Adam and Eve allow themselves to be distracted
from an awareness of God's presence, because they didn't
ask if God was in the suggestion, they engage in conversation with the serpent.
They listen to it.
'Did God really say . . .?'

Introducing doubt about God.
As do the distractions with which we engage. They make
us look away from God. And, as we do, doubts creep in:
'Did God really say . . .?'
Is that really true?

JEHOVAH RAAH (The Lord My Shepherd)
God looks after me. All the time.
Is that really true?
It's in the Bible:

> *He tends his flock like a shepherd: he gathers the lambs*
> *in his arms and carries them close to his heart; he gently*
> *leads those that have young.*
>
> Isaiah 40:11

JEHOVAH SHAMMAH (The Lord Is There)
Wherever I am, God is.
Is that really true?
It's in the Bible:

*The LORD Almighty is with us; the God of Jacob is our fortress.*

Psalm 46:7

JEHOVAH TSIDKENU (The Lord Our Righteousness)
God deals with the bad things in me.
Is that really true?
It's in the Bible:

*God made him who had no sin to be sin for us, so that in him we might become the righteousness of God.*

2 Corinthians 5:21

JEHOVAH SHALOM (The Lord Is Peace)
God is peace for my days.
Is that really true?
It's in the Bible:

*He himself is our peace.*
Ephesians 2:14

Father God
Everywhere I am, you are.
Help me remember to focus.
Always.
Amen

Adam and Eve's response is to try to solve their problem themselves.

They'd realized they were naked and didn't like it, so they sewed leaves into clothes.

'I can't see me, so I'm not here . . .'

What clothes do we sew for ourselves? Things to try to cover up things in us we don't want seen?

Masks to hide behind.

I had prayer for healing once. Beforehand, I got 'dressed' carefully. The clothes I chose to put on were bravado and 'knowing best'. I refused to believe that I wouldn't be healed. I even told people that, after this meeting, I would be able to hear. I wouldn't be deaf any more. If there was a little voice inside that knew I would be deaf, I quickly put clothes on it. I hid it.

I couldn't – or wouldn't – see it, so it wasn't there.

I knelt down, wrapping my clothes around me. Some-one came and began to pray. And I realized God was there . . .

As Adam and Eve, wrapped in their self-made clothes, re-alize that God is there.

Self-made clothes are transparent before God.

For me, in that moment, with all my self-made clothes stripped away, I felt one thing. Joy.

*You make known to me the path of life; you will fill me*
*with joy in your presence, with eternal pleasures at your*
*right hand.*

Psalm 16:11

I knew, without a doubt, that I would not be healed that
day. Maybe never will be.
But I also knew something bigger than that.
I knew joy.
Because God was there.
Find God, know joy.

Father God
The joy you give me is so great.
Yet there's more?
Evermore?
Amen

God asks: **Where are you?**
He knows the answer.
But he asks anyway.
**Where are you?**

How would you answer that question? Not 'at home' or
'sitting in a chair' but 'in an angry place' or 'in a scared
place' or 'in a confused place' or . . .

Father God
Let me tell you where I am . . .
Amen

Into Adam and Eve's hiding places, God comes.

Close enough to call.

**Where are you?**

So we answered him. Well, Adam did. He said, 'I heard you in the garden and I was scared, because I'm naked. So I hid.'[4] I thought God might be angry with us, but to be honest, when he spoke, he sounded more sad than angry. He said, 'Who told you that you were naked?'[5]

In other words, 'Who told you that who I made you to be is not enough?'
**You're made in my image.**
**You're special.**
**You're mine.**

> *God created mankind in his own image, in the image of God he created them; male and female he created them.*
> Genesis 1:27

If God made everyone in his image, the image of God is in everyone.
Every person on this planet captures something of the essence of God. However frustrating they may be, they carry God's image.

Do you see God's image in other people? Do you see his image in you?
You'll find it if you take time to look.

God knows everything about you.
You're made in his image.
You are enough.

Father God
Help me believe I am enough.
Amen

'It was her!' That brought me up short. I'm the only 'her' around here. Adam was blaming me for us eating the fruit. It was a new thing, to feel cross with him. But I did. It wasn't fair that he was blaming me. When God asked me, 'What is this you have done?'[6] I felt awful. I was so ashamed. Then I realized I could do what Adam had. I told God, 'No, it was the snake. It tricked me'. And God punished all three of us.

'They started it!' 'I only did it because they did!'
Children the world over say these things. Like Adam and Eve, they pass the blame.

What about adults? There are pressures in today's world. Pressure to do what others are doing. Pressure to keep up. Pressure to have what others have, be what others are.

Sometimes that is good. It's good to have role models, people to emulate. But sometimes it is not so good. We start comparing. And we end up thinking we need to be something we are not.

In John 21, Jesus and Peter are discussing Peter's life. What he'll do, where he'll go.

Suddenly, Peter changes the subject. He sees John, and says to Jesus: 'What about him? What about his life?' And Jesus responds, 'What is that to you? You must follow me.'[7]

**Don't compare. Just follow me.**

'I only did it because they did.'

What about 'They only did it because I did'?

The apostle Paul addressed this. He recognized that people in the church watched him and were guided by him. And he took the responsibility seriously, as Romans 14 shows.

Paul himself had come to a place before God which allowed him to eat any food he chose. He didn't regard it as 'unclean'. Others, he knew, did regard some food as unclean and, because they did, Paul would not eat that food in their presence. He didn't want people to do something unhelpful to them and then say 'I only did it because you did'.

> *If your brother or sister is distressed because of what you eat, you are no longer acting in love.*
> *Do not by your eating destroy someone for whom Christ died.*
>
> v. 15

To be distressed means to feel hurt or anxiety or sadness.

Sometimes, Christians can cause anxiety to other Christians. Anxiety that they don't seem as all-out for God as other believers. They don't preach, or teach children. They seem to find it harder to resist temptations.

Eating is an action. It's something we do.
'If your brother or sister is distressed because of what you [do], you are no longer acting in love.'
As people watch you, and are perhaps guided by you, how seriously do you take the responsibility?

Father God
May I impart love,
not distress.
Amen

'Do not by your eating destroy someone for whom Christ died.'

This verse would have originally been written in Greek, and the word translated 'destroy' refers to deliberate evasion. Avoidance. Being distant.
Do not make yourself distant from someone for whom Christ died. If you do, you're not acting in love.
Challenging stuff!

Since Paul is talking about eating, we might conclude that he is referring to specific times when the church came together for fellowship. Times when the church was physically together.
When you are together, don't be distant.

When we come together as brothers and sisters in Christ, could we be described as making ourselves remote from each other? Far apart in relationship? Avoiding each other?

Being sure not to talk to her, harbouring resentments against him, seething with anger about something someone did, never sitting with certain people.

Do not make yourself distant from someone for whom Christ died. If you do, you're not acting in love.

*Dear friends, let us love one another, for love comes from God.*

1 John 4:7

Father God
Help me to show love to others.
Love that wants the best for them.
Real love.
Amen

When God asked who told us we were naked, before we could answer, he asked another question. Had we eaten fruit from the tree he'd told us not to? At first, I didn't know why he didn't expect an answer about the nakedness. But now, I think it's because the first question wasn't really to do with us. It was to do with external influence. Words coming at us. But the second question was to do with internal influence. Our decision. We didn't have to eat the fruit, even though we'd been told we could. We chose to eat it.

External influence. It happens a lot. Maybe, in some ways in this passage, God is saying, 'It's not your fault. It's not your fault that this was said to you. It's not your fault you were offered the fruit. It's not your responsibility.'

Sometimes we are exposed to things we shouldn't have heard, or seen. Or things are said to us that shouldn't be said. And that is not our fault.

Don't take on too much responsibility for someone else's words or actions.

> *Nothing outside a person can defile them by going into them. Rather, it is what comes out of a person that defiles them.*
>
> Mark 7:15

We are responsible for our own actions, words, deeds.
Eve had a choice. She didn't have to take that fruit, but she did.
We can't always choose our circumstances, but we can choose how we respond to them.

> *Yet you desired faithfulness even in the womb; you taught me wisdom in that secret place.*
>
> Psalm 51:6

Father God
Help me make wise choices.
Amen

Adam and Eve stood there in their home-made clothes. And, before God, those clothes became meaningless.

All that mattered to God was them. He didn't even mention the clothes they'd made. The covering they'd made to hide who they were didn't hide them from him. He knew them. As he knows you.

> *You have searched me, LORD, and you know me. For you created my inmost being; you knit me together in my mother's womb.*
>
> Psalm 139:1,13

God also knew their circumstances. He knew that they now struggled with their nakedness. And, in his grace, he replaced their clothes with clothes he made himself.[8]

Adam and Eve were wearing home-made clothes.
And God gave them grace-made clothes.

**Where are you?**
*I'm hiding.*
**Where are you?**
*I'm not telling you.*
*I'm not.*
*I won't.*
*I can't.*
*I can't tell you where I am.*
*I don't know where I am.*
*I only know I'm hiding.*
**I'll tell you where you are.**
**You're in a made-in-my-image place.**
*No, I'm not.*

*I was, once.*
*But now I'm hiding.*
*Life is hard.*
*I think bad thoughts.*
**You're in a made-in-my-image place.**
*Today I lost my temper.*
*Yesterday I grumbled and moaned.*
*I said it's not fair.*
**You're in a made-in-my-image place.**
*No, I'm not.*
*I was, once.*
*But now I'm far away from you.*
**You're in a made-in-my-image place.**
*I'm not. I'm scared. I don't want you to see me like this.*
**You don't want me to see my image?**
*There's nothing to see.*
**Can I be the judge of that? Let me look at you.**
*Not yet, just wait. I need to get changed.*
*Attitude-changed.*
*Everything-changed.*
*After that, maybe there'll be something to see.*
**No there won't.**
**If you change everything about you, my image won't be there.**
**You're in a made-in-my-image place.**
**My image is in you.**
**Right now.**
*But right now I'm struggling.*
*I don't know where I am.*

*I'm feeling low.*
*I don't recognize myself.*
**I recognize you, my child.**
**I see my image in you.**
**I do.**
**You're in a made-in-my-image place.**

*God created mankind in his own image,*
*in the image of God he created them;*
*male and female he created them.*
                              Genesis 1:27

Father God
So often, I allow other things in my life to be more
                important than you.
I don't mean to.
They just take over, until they've pushed you into second
                place.
Maybe even third or fourth place, if I'm honest.
I hide behind them.
Hiding you from me.
And I realize joy is missing.
Because you are missing.
Help me to turn my back on anything that will come
                between me and you.
Thank you that you know me.
I never need to hide from you.
                Amen

**REFLECTION**

- What causes you to look away from God?
- What clothes do you sew as a covering for yourself?
- Where do you see God's image in yourself?
- What example are you setting others as you live your life?

**GOD'S CALLING CARD**

# 2

# Hagar
(Genesis 16; 21)

 *The angel of God called to Hagar from heaven and said to her, 'What is the matter, Hagar?'*
Genesis 21:17

When I was 16, I was told I'd one day lose my hearing. My mum's response was, 'We'd better go and learn sign language.' So we did. We worked hard at it, but it still took a long time to become anywhere near passable. A long time until we were able to hold a simple conversation in sign language. And it was exhausting! I remember the first time I attempted to understand a professional sign language interpreter. It was at a Christian conference and, for weeks beforehand, I'd been praying that I'd at least understand some of what was signed. In the event, I did understand, but I confess I can't now remember much of what was said. I recall one thing, though. The topic was 'Holding on to God'. I wondered how this would be interpreted in sign language. As I watched, the interpreter simply reached her open hand upwards, in 'God's direction'. Then she closed her hand, as though holding on to something. Holding on to God . . .

I'm pregnant. When I found out, I went straight to tell Sarai. She can't have children herself, so told Abram, her husband, to have them with me instead. But the thing is, when I saw her, I thought – for the first time since I became her servant – that I had something over her. I was expecting Abram's baby. And for some reason, that made me despise Sarai. As the baby grew inside me, so did my lack of respect for my mistress. Sarai saw this and began treating me really badly. I thought Abram would support me, but no. He didn't. I was carrying his child yet he still preferred Sarai. In the end, it was all too much and I ran away. So here I am, in the desert. On my own. I thought people might come looking for me. I even sat near a spring and a road, but no one came. Then an angel from God arrived. He told me to go back to Sarai and submit to her . . .

The angel of God, who caused Hagar to name God 'the Living One who sees me', told Hagar what to name her son when he was born.
Ishmael: 'God hears'.

As she sat, alone, in the desert, Hagar was reminded that God sees. God saw her, when no one else did. God heard her misery, when no one else did.

God doesn't change.
He still sees us when no one else does.
Hears us when no one else does.

*Do not fear, for I have redeemed you; I have summoned you by name; you are mine. When you pass through the waters, I will be with you; and when you pass through the rivers, they will not sweep over you. When you walk through the fire, you will not be burned; the flames will not set you ablaze.*

Isaiah 43:1,2

So I went back. And if I felt invisible, I remembered I wasn't invisible to God. If I felt no one listened to me, I remembered that God did. My baby grew inside me, and with every flutter as he turned, Ishmael reminded me that God sees me.

What reminds you that God sees you? What gives you the courage to reach up and hold on to God? The God who sees you. The God who is right there.

*And because we are his children, God has sent the Spirit of his Son into our hearts, prompting us to call out, 'Abba, Father.'*

Galatians 4:6, NLT

The Spirit of God. Indwelling. Reminding us that we have permission to call out to God. More than reminding us. Prompting us.

God's Spirit actually encourages us to call out to God. And, since God gave us this encouraging Spirit, it's safe to conclude that he wants us to call out to him.

The God we call out to is like the best-ever daddy. *Abba*. He cares. He sees. He's right here. Hold on.

*You are precious and honoured in my sight . . . I love you.*
                                                Isaiah 43:4


Father God
Thank you that you see me.
Right now.
Wherever I am,
you always see me.
Amen


Ishmael was born and things were not bad. Until Sarai became pregnant. She was really old! But she had a son, Isaac. At the baby's weaning party, I saw something that made my blood run cold. It was like looking in a mirror. Remember how I despised Sarai before? Well, I saw Ishmael being mean to the baby: laughing at him, mocking him.


What do people learn from watching you? What do you pass on?

It has been said that actions speak louder than words. Perhaps, in some ways, sign language combines the two. When I sign, I use actions to convey meaning. Once, as my 6-year-old niece stood beside me in church, singing, I became aware of her arms moving. I looked down and saw that she was looking up at me. She was copying my actions as I signed. Perhaps she didn't understand the actions at first. But, as she paired those actions with the words she was hearing sung, they gained meaning for her.

Actions gave extra meaning to words.

The same can be true of the Christian life. We can say the right thing, but do our lives back it up? When we leave church and head into our week, can people see that, because of Jesus, we are different?

Do our actions give extra meaning to the God we profess to follow?

God, who is 'compassionate and gracious, slow to anger, abounding in love' (Ps. 103:8).

Do our actions and behaviour point to God?


> Father God
> May my heart and actions be
> compassionate. Like you.
> Gracious. Like you.
> Slow to anger. Like you.
> Abounding in love. Like you.
> Amen


A child was weaned at the age of 2 or 3 in the Ancient Near East. Isaac would have known Ishmael was mocking. He was young, but not oblivious.

Add to that the fact that Isaac was a child of the promise.[1] Chosen by God. Mocked by his brother.

How do we treat people young in faith? Those whom God has chosen (1 Pet. 2:9)?

Are they, like Isaac, chosen by God yet sidelined by their brothers and sisters?

*Don't let anyone look down on you because you are young, but set an example for the believers in speech, in conduct, in love, in faith and in purity.*

1 Timothy 4:12

Here Paul tells Timothy not to allow people to disregard him because he's young, which implies that people are looking down on him, or that there is potential for them to do so.

Do you have potential to look down on people? To feel superior to them? To disregard them because they do things differently?

Father God
Help me not to do that.
Amen

Then Paul tells Timothy to set an example for people who are older than him. The older still have things to learn.

However old we are in faith years, there is always more to learn. The more we know of God, the more we have to know.

One of the most powerful lessons about prayer I have learned was from the example of a child. My godson. (Coincidentally, he's called Isaac!) When 'my' Isaac was 2 years old, he was encouraged to pray at bedtime, just before he went to sleep.

At that age, he knew what prayer was. It was talking to God/Jesus. The thing was, he didn't have the language skills to say very much. One night, he wanted to pray for his grandma. Three words were enough.

'Jesus
Grandma
Amen'

> *[Jesus] called a little child to him, and placed the child among them. And he said: 'Truly I tell you, unless you change and become like little children, you will never enter the kingdom of heaven.'*
>
> Matthew 18:2,3

Sometimes, like my godson, we struggle to find language for our prayers. Hopes, fears, dreams, frustrations. Our hearts are bursting with things we can't express.

> *. . . your Father knows what you need . . .*
> Matthew 6:8

Know that your Father God knows.

Jesus
Me
Amen

Today Abraham gave me food and water, then sent Ishmael and me away. I don't think he wanted to, but God told him to.

And what God says, Abraham does, even though traditionally it is wrong to send Ishmael away. Ishmael is nineteen years old now, and he and I went off into the desert.

God told Abraham (formerly called Abram) to remove Ishmael and Hagar. They weren't helpful in terms of God's plan, which was that many people would be blessed through Isaac, not Ishmael.

Galatians 4 tells us that while Ishmael was the child of a slave woman, Isaac was the child of a free woman. And God's promise is freedom. That's why Isaac was allowed to stay, while Ishmael left. Slavery and freedom are opposites. But how often we let them co-exist in our lives. And, when we do, slavery becomes more and more present. And we become more and more trapped and enslaved by things that shouldn't even be there:

'I need to do this, and be this, and tick these boxes in order to be accepted by God.'

> *Rid yourselves of all malice and all deceit, hypocrisy, envy, and slander of every kind.*
>
> 1 Peter 2:1

As children of God's promised freedom, these things in 1 Peter 2 have no right to be part of us.
Yet, like the snake in the garden of Eden, they worm their way in, threatening – even ruining – the freedom we can enjoy in God.
Rid yourself of them . . .

The word translated 'rid' carries the meaning of 'throw off'.
Take deliberate action. It's difficult to throw something off accidently.
For me, deliberate action starts with telling the devil to get lost.
Did God really say you should get rid of slander? Well, yes, he did. In the Bible. Through Peter. So get lost, devil!

Get rid of spreading any lies and hurtful things about people.
Don't do it. Get lost, devil!
And get rid of believing lies and hurtful things about yourself.
Don't do it. Get lost, devil!

God offers you freedom.
Freedom to be who he made you to be.
His beloved.

Father God
Rule over my lips and thoughts.
May I only speak truth and good
about others,
and about myself.
Amen

So, Ishmael would not be helpful in terms of God's covenant plan. Do you have things in your life that aren't helpful in terms of God's plan?
What is God's plan?
Well, it will look different for everyone. We are all different, and that's good.

*But in fact God has placed the parts in the body, every one of them, just as he wanted them to be.*

1 Corinthians 12:18

But we are all differently placed into one body. The body of Christ. The details of our individual lives may look different, but we are united. We have a shared plan from God that he longs for each member of his body to live by:

*He has shown you, O mortal, what is good. And what does the LORD require of you? To act justly and to love mercy and to walk humbly with your God.*

Micah 6:8

Act justly.
Do the right thing, even when it's tough.
Love mercy.
Mercy can be defined as 'not getting what we deserve'.
We live in a world which focuses very much on what we deserve. We are told through advertising, the media in general, and other people, that we deserve so much.
Actually, we don't deserve any of it.

*For it is by grace you have been saved, through faith – and this is not from yourselves, it is the gift of God – not by works, so that no one can boast.*

Ephesians 2:8,9

Walk humbly.
Not 'run ahead' humbly. Not 'stand still' humbly. Not 'go backwards' humbly.

Walk. Step by step with God.
One foot in front of the other, with God.

School sports days traditionally have a three-legged race.
One person ties their left leg to another person's right leg,
and then the two of them attempt to walk. If one person
refuses to move, or tries to run without checking the other
is alongside, the pair will not reach the finishing line.
But, if they work together, every step, they will reach their
goal.
Humility is our goal. And if we are walking in step with
God, we will achieve it.
Wherever those steps take us.

> *Now Moses was a very humble man, more humble than
> anyone else on the face of the earth.*
>
> Numbers 12:3

Let's just think about what Moses did:
He led more than a million people through the desert. He
helped them, he managed them, he told them off if needs
be. He had authority. God performed miracles through
him. People looked to him for guidance.
Yet he was a humble man.
Something that stands out in Moses' story is how often he
'tied his leg' to God's. He talked things through with God.
Importantly, he didn't want to go where God wasn't.

> *Then Moses said to him, 'If your Presence does not go
> with us, do not send us up from here.'*
>
> Exodus 33:15

When was the last time you checked that you're walking in step with God?
Tie yourself to him.
That's all that's required.
Tie yourself to him.
Remember that his presence is what enables you.
And 'walk humbly with your God'.

Father God
Help me to tie my leg to yours.
Amen

We walked and walked, and eventually our water ran out. We had nothing to drink. I knew we were going to die. I looked at Ishmael. He was so thirsty. It broke my heart. How could I possibly just watch him die? He sat down. I left him under a bush and I went a short way off and sat down, too. I could hear Ishmael crying. I began to cry. And that's when I heard a voice. Calling. From heaven.

Close enough to call.

> *God heard the boy crying, and the angel of God called to Hagar from heaven and said to her, 'What is the matter, Hagar? Do not be afraid; God has heard the boy crying as he lies there. Lift the boy up and take him by the hand, for I will make him into a great nation.'*
>
> Genesis 21:17,18

Into Hagar's despair, God calls.
'What is the matter?'

**What's wrong, Hagar? I know something is on your mind. And I care.**
**Enough to ask.**
**Enough to want to share it.**
'Do not be afraid.'
**Don't be scared. I'm here.**
'God has heard.'
**I heard your boy crying. I heard your heart-cry.**
**I care.**

*You keep track of all my sorrows. You have collected all my tears in your bottle. You have recorded each one in your book.*

Psalm 56:8, NLT

Hagar didn't need to say anything.
God knew her heart.
God knows your heart.
Hold on.

*But when I am afraid, I will put my trust in you. I praise God for what he has promised. I trust in God, so why should I be afraid? What can mere mortals do to me?*

Psalm 56:3,4, NLT

Father God
I'm holding on to you.
Amen

Hagar clothed herself in despair. She could see no way forward.

I was lying on a hospital bed, being wheeled down a hospital corridor that led to theatre. In the last four years, I had undergone five major brain surgeries and I'd lost count of the more minor surgeries. The minor tally was about to grow. I had discovered a comparatively small lump on my leg, which needed to be surgically removed. The doctors assured me it would be an easy surgery. I wouldn't even need to stay in hospital overnight. Excellent news.

Yet, as I lay on that bed, being pushed down a seemingly endless corridor, something inside me snapped.
Suddenly, I'd had enough. What was I doing in hospital, again? How was this my life? My life was not supposed to feature operations and hospitals. It would be better if I had no life at all.

I said to God: 'Don't let me wake up from this anaesthetic.'
And God said, **You'll wake up.**
**Your life is not over yet.**
As the bed took me closer to the theatre which would be part of, rather than the end of, my life, my heart whispered to God: 'But how can I keep living this life?'
**Emily, you do need to let go. But not of life. You need to let go of what you thought life would be. So you can accept what it is.**
Let go.

Like me, Hagar needed to let go. Not of life, but of what she'd expected life to be.

Life no longer held the hope of her son being with his father. But that didn't mean there was no hope.

*'For I know the plans I have for you,' declares the LORD, 'plans to prosper you and not to harm you, plans to give you hope and a future.'*

Jeremiah 29:11

Help is at hand.
There is always hope.
Hold on.

Father God
In my hopelessness, please
show me your hope.
Amen

Hagar clothed herself in despair.
And God clothed her in assurance.
Assurance that Ishmael would live.
Assurance that he would become a great nation.
Assurance that she could take the first step:
Hagar, 'Lift the boy up and take him by the hand.'
One step at a time.

However low we feel, God promises us a future.
Which means we can go on.
And step one? Let God lift us up and take us by the hand.
No more than that.
Just be lifted and held by God.

'What is the matter?'
'Do not be afraid.'
'God has heard.'

> *For I am the* LORD *your God who takes hold of your*
> *right hand and says to you,*
> *Do not fear; I will help you.*

Isaiah 41:13

*I am seen.*
*In the wilderness of life,*
*beside streams of provision*
*or far from them,*
*I am seen.*
*I forget that I'm seen.*
*By the stream,*
*when I have what I need*
*but things don't feel so good*
*and I long to be noticed (really noticed – by someone –*
*anyone),*
*I forget that I'm seen.*
*Far from the stream,*
*I don't have what I need.*
*Trouble looms.*
*I'm all alone.*
*I want it to end.*
*I forget that I'm seen.*
*Seen by the One who sees everything.*
*The One who sees through.*
*Sees through the smile to my despair.*

*Sees through to the silent screams behind my coping.*
*Who knows me inside out,*
*yet never looks away.*
*I am seen.*
*Being seen, I dare return his gaze.*
*And I live in his seeing.*
*By the stream.*
*In the wilderness.*
*I live seen.*

*The eyes of the LORD are on those who fear him, on those whose hope is in his unfailing love.*

Psalm 33:18

Father God
I am in a wilderness.
So often, I run here.
I don't know why.
I just need to escape.
But the wilderness is empty.
It's not all I thought it would be.
It doesn't help me.
But you do.
My God, who stays with me in the wilderness,
then gently leads me out.
Holding me fast.
Amen

## REFLECTION

- What reminds you that you are seen by God?
- If people copied you, would they be living God's way?
- What do you need to throw off to get to freedom? How will you throw it off?
- Do you need to let go of things?
- What makes you afraid? How can you trust it to God?
- Think of a situation you'd like to pray for. Narrow it down to one word.

## GOD'S CALLING CARD

# 3

# Abraham
(Genesis 22)

 *The angel of the LORD called out to him from heaven, 'Abraham! Abraham!'*

v. 11

If I had to describe my 2-year-old niece in one word, it would be 'happy'. Elianne radiates happiness and joy for life. She spreads it wherever she goes. Her catchphrase is: 'Here I am!' She'll walk into a room and, despite the fact that everyone can see her, announce, 'Here I am!' Or into the garden: 'Here I am!' Or kitchen: 'Here I am!' Or anywhere: 'Here I am!' Because why wouldn't everyone be delighted to see her? It (rightly) doesn't occur to her that her presence will not bring joy. Here I am . . .

Every time I look at Isaac, I feel a sense of amazement that he's here at all. I love him more than I thought possible. God promised Sarah would give me a son. I believed him. I really did. But when Sarah suggested I have a child through Hagar, I thought perhaps that was the way. Then years later, God said to me that Sarah would give me a son. I must admit I laughed at that. Sarah was 90 years old! But that was about twenty years ago.

Twenty years of watching Isaac grow, of getting to know him, of feeling overwhelmingly blessed.

God promised Abram a son (and changed his name to Abraham).[1]

A promise is more than a hope, or a vague plan, or a dream. It's a declaration of absolute certainty.

God declared to Abraham that he would have a child. Abraham believed God, but thought he'd better help put the plan into action. He'd found out what God wanted, but thought he'd sort out the details himself.
The difference between belief and trust.
Abraham believed God's promise would happen, he just didn't quite trust enough to hand the 'how' over to God.
Perhaps he believed in his heart but not in his head. Heart belief not head belief. His head asked 'How?'

In Mark 9, Jesus encounters a boy who was possessed by an impure spirit, which made him deaf and mute. His father had asked Jesus' disciples to heal the boy, but they couldn't do it. Then Jesus comes along. And the father turns to him instead: 'If you can help him, please do.' Jesus had already healed a deaf and mute man[2] and they may well have known about this. But, perhaps due to the human inability the man had seen in the disciples, a bit of doubt is planted in his mind. So 'if you can' heal him . . . He should have known Jesus could heal. He did know. But his head allowed room for doubt.

And Jesus picked him up on it. 'If you can?' In other words, are you questioning the ability of the Creator of the universe?

> *'"If you can"?' said Jesus. 'Everything is possible for one who believes.'*
>
> Mark 9:23

Immediately the boy's father exclaimed, 'I do believe; help me overcome my unbelief!' (v. 24).
I do believe, help me overcome that bit within my belief that struggles to trust.

Abraham laughed at God's promise. He laughed because there were reasons the promise seemed impossible.

> *Jesus looked at them and said, 'With man this is impossible, but with God all things are possible.'*
>
> Matthew 19:26

How do you respond to God's promises? Do you have a laughter equivalent? Something that shows you gauge the promise impossible? You can't quite trust it?

Sometimes, trust is difficult because our trust has been betrayed by people. Someone we trusted has let us down.
God's not like that. He'll never let us down. Ever.
Maybe we need to get to a place that reminds us that God is not like people who've hurt us.
Maybe we are not there yet.

But that doesn't mean we never will be.

> *God is not human, that he should lie, not a human be-*
> *ing, that he should change his mind. Does he speak and*
> *then not act? Does he promise and not fulfil?*
>
> Numbers 23:19

Father God
I do believe.
Please help me overcome the bit of me
that struggles to trust you with the how.
Amen

A few days ago, God said, 'Abraham!' and I replied, 'Here I am', and then God said something that made me wish I *wasn't* here. He told me to take Isaac, my son whom I love, to a mountain he would tell me about and kill him as a sacrifice. *Kill my son?* So the next morning, I set off with Isaac. I didn't tell Isaac where we were going, but I knew. And God knew.

Things are going well. Abraham is blessed by God. He has a son who is his pride and joy. God is with him. God speaks to him. Life is good. Is it any wonder that the minute God spoke his name, Abraham answered 'Here I am'?

'Here' meant surrounded by good things.
But 'here' was about to change.
'Here' became confusion: why would God want me to kill Isaac?
'Here' became doing what he didn't want to do.
'Here' became going where he didn't want to go.

Circumstances changed.
Drastically.

But in the 'here' that Abraham would never have chosen, he still obeyed God. He didn't run the other way as fast as he could, dragging Isaac with him.
No.
He went to the place God had told him about. And God went with him.

Maybe you're in a 'here' you wouldn't choose.
When I was 16, newly diagnosed with brain tumours and awaiting surgery, God spoke to my mum. He said, 'The operation will go well, but will be followed by complications. Things will be difficult.'
We'd be in a 'here' we didn't want.
The 'here' led to my mum being asked permission to switch off my life support machine. When, at the eleventh hour, that decision became unnecessary, 'here' became months of rehabilitation in hospital.

For sixteen years, my 'here' had, by and large, been good.
'Here I am!'
But 'here' changed. I was in a difficult place. 'Here I am.'

Echoes from Eden: '**Where are you?**'
Sometimes, 'here' is all I know.
I don't know where here is.
But it's where I am.
And God knows where my here is.
God knows where your here is.

Tell him.
**'Where are you?'**
'Here I am.'

> *When you pass through the waters,*
> *I will be with you;*
> *and when you pass through the rivers,*
> *they will not sweep over you.*
> *When you walk through the fire,*
> *you will not be burned;*
> *the flames will not set you ablaze.*

Isaiah 43:2

God never leaves our 'here'. Not for a single second.
**Where are you?**

Father God
Here I am.
Amen

Abraham's love and faith were tested. God knew how much Abraham loved Isaac. But did Abraham love Isaac more than he loved God?

> *You have persevered and have endured hardships for my*
> *name, and have not grown weary.*
> *Yet I hold this against you: you have forsaken the love*
> *you had at first.*

Revelation 2:3,4

Abraham had certainly persevered, and endured hardships. He'd been called to leave his home. He'd had to ask his son, Ishmael, to leave the family. He'd split from his nephew. And through it all, he'd carried on. His faith hadn't wavered. His love for God was strong.

Yet:

> *Take your son . . . whom you love . . . and [kill] him.*
>                                         Genesis 22:2

Years before (see Gen. 12), God had asked Abraham to give up the life he knew: for God. God said to Abraham, **Go to the place I'll show you.**

Not: 'Have a look at the map and I'll point out exactly where you are going.'

**Go to the place I'll show you.**

And Abraham went. He was obedient. God's knowing was enough.

Is God's knowing enough for you?

And then comes another test. **Kill your son.**

Would God's knowing still be enough? Or had some of Abraham's initial faith faded?

Abraham's circumstances had changed. He now had a child. Had this important addition to his life affected Abraham's love for God?

> *Yet I hold this against you: you have forsaken the love you had at first.*
>                                         Revelation 2:4

Could it be said of you that you've forsaken the love you had at first for God?

Life takes over and pushes God into second place?

In a sense, God was asking Abraham: **Would you give up everything for me?**

Paul said:

> *But whatever were gains to me I now consider loss for the sake of Christ. What is more, I consider everything a loss because of the surpassing worth of knowing Christ Jesus my Lord, for whose sake I have lost all things. I consider them garbage, that I may gain Christ.*
>
> Philippians 3:7,8

I'm often asked if I'd like to hear again. The answer is 'yes'! I would love to hear again. Somehow, though, I can never stop there. I always add *but only if it's what God wants.*

So far, it's not what God wants. I am still deaf.

For me, were I to stop at 'yes, I want to hear again', I would be forsaking the love I had for God. The love that said, 'I don't need to know the whys, I just need to know you're with me.'

I was recently asked how I square a loving God with the suffering I've been through:

> *If God is love – and I believe he is – why should I let my circumstances affect his ability to love? He's bigger than that. His love is bigger than that. I don't think it's fair for me to say, do it my way and I'll believe you love me, but lead me on a path I don't like and I will know that you*

*don't love me. I mean, how would that make sense? God
is God, I am not; how can I even begin to dictate to him.*[3]

Whatever else happens, 'God is love'.

*And so we know and rely on the love God has for us.*
1 John 4:16

God is love.
Know it.
Rely on it.
God loved Abraham.
God loves me.
God loves you.

Father God
May my heart overflow with love
from you.
Amen

When we were nearly there, Isaac wanted to know where the lamb
for the sacrifice was. It was a fair point. He knew we had fire and
wood. After all, we were carrying it. I told him God would provide
the lamb, and we carried on walking. Isaac didn't ask me about
the lamb again.

Jehovah Jireh: God will provide.

God will provide. Full stop. And that was enough for Isaac.
It was all he needed to know.

God will provide. Isaac didn't even ask how. He believed that God could, and that God would.

Is 'God will provide, full stop' enough for you?

In 1 Kings 17, Elijah needs somewhere to stay. He arrives at the town of Zarephath, sees a woman gathering sticks, and asks her for some food. She says she can't, she doesn't have much to give. All she has is the final meal she plans to eat with her son before they die. There's no more food.

Elijah says, 'You'll be alright. Give me some food first, bring it to me, and then make something for you and your son. God says that until this famine ends, your food jar will never be empty.'

In other words, you'll always have enough.

Jehovah Jireh: God will provide.

> Father God
> Thank you for making sure
> I always have enough.
> Amen

Abraham had a choice. Stick with God, even though it was hard. Or go the other way.

He stuck with God.

Find where God is. And be there, too.

*. . . you will fill me with joy in your presence . . .*

Psalm 16:11

Sometimes 'fill me with joy' is translated 'fullness of joy'.[4]
There have been times in my life that have been difficult.
There still are. I often feel like a victim of my circumstances,
carried along on a wave I didn't want to catch. But that
doesn't mean I don't have a choice. I always have a choice.
Will I invite God to ride the waves of my life with me,
or not? I can't change my circumstances, but I can choose
whether I face them alone or with God at my side. And
I would rather be with God than without him.
Every time.

*Here I am.*

*When you pass through the waters,*
*I will be with you;*
*and when you pass through the rivers,*
*they will not sweep over you.*
*When you walk through the fire,*
*you will not be burned;*
*the flames will not set you ablaze.*

Isaiah 43:2

We've reached the mountain God told me to go to now. Isaac is
amazing. He didn't ask about the lamb again, even when he saw me
building an altar. Even when I asked him to pass me the wood he'd
carried, to go on top of the altar. Even when I couldn't put the

moment off any longer, so tied Isaac up and laid him on the altar. Not a word of protest. And I know he's stronger than me. He didn't have to be tied up, he let me do it.

Here we have a foreshadowing of Jesus going to the cross.
He, too, carried wood.
He, too, was bound.
He, too, remained silent.
He did it for me.
And he did it for you.

Father God
Thank you for Jesus.
Amen

I raised the knife over Isaac. Over my son. A split second before I killed him, I heard a voice. The angel of the Lord, calling from heaven.

Close enough to call.

'Abraham! Abraham!' The angel told me not to do anything to Isaac. Now he knew I feared God, because I didn't hold anything back from him, even my son. I looked up and I saw a ram with its horns tangled in a bush. I sacrificed it instead of Isaac.

Into Abraham's steadfast obedience, the angel of God – who sometimes seems to be God himself in the Old Testament – calls.
God is a God of compassion.
A God of grace.

*My grace is sufficient for you, for my power is made per-
fect in weakness.*

2 Corinthians 12:9

You will always have enough.

God's grace never runs out. There's never no more grace.

**Abraham, sacrifice a ram instead of your son.**

**My compassion makes provision.**

Did God look through time to when such grace would not
be offered to him?

Abraham was faced with a difficult thing. Kill his son. And
he would have done it. He got as far as raising the knife.
Had he gone through with it, he'd have been obeying God.
God had told him what to do, and he was doing it.

Abraham never stopped being obedient. But he learned
that God doesn't issue orders from afar and then leave us
to get on with it. He is with us in our obedience.

Abraham clothed himself with obedience.

God called into that obedience: 'Abraham! Abraham!'

**I'm here, too.**

And he clothed Abraham with provision.

**I'm your God of compassion.**

**I'm your God of grace.**

As we live whatever life God has given us, in obedience to
him, he's there, too.

> *He gives strength to the weary*
> *and increases the power of the weak.*
> *Even youths grow tired and weary,*

*and young men stumble and fall;*
*but those who hope in the* LORD
*will renew their strength.*
*They will soar on wings like eagles;*
*they will run and not grow weary,*
*they will walk and not be faint.*

Isaiah 40:29–31

*Here I am!*
**Here I am!**
*Why are you copying me?*
*I'm trying to tell you I'm here.*
*Here I am!*
**I know you are.**
**Here I am!**
**I'm here, too.**
*I know you are.*
*It gives me joy.*
*'In your presence there is joy.'*
**That's not what it says, though, is it?**
*Well, almost. It actually says 'fullness of joy',[5] but . . .*
**Don't you want fullness of joy?**
*Isn't that the same thing as joy?*
*The joy of knowing you're there?*
**Your delight in my presence is joy.**
**Fullness of joy is even more.**
**It's knowing that you give me joy.**
**Mutual joy.**
*Oh. I don't experience fullness of joy.*
**I know, my child. But tell me, why?**
*Because I'm not a joy-giver, because I'm me.*

**Well, that's strange.**
**I'm a joy-receiver, because of you.**
**How is that possible, if you don't give joy?**
*It's not possible.*
*But everything is possible with you.*
*Do you mean it?*
*You're a joy-receiver because of me?*
**I mean it.**
*Here I am!*
**Here I am!**
Fullness of joy.

> *[I am] with you, [I am] the Mighty Warrior who saves.*
> *[I] take great delight in you; [I calm you with my]*
> *love . . . [I] rejoice over you with singing.*
>                                        Zephaniah 3:17

Father God
Why do I sometimes doubt?
Your promises are true.
I know that.
Yet I struggle to trust what I know.
Struggle to really believe it.
Please come to me, in your grace,
in your compassion,
and help me trust.
Really trust.
I always have enough.
Not because of myself, but
because of you.
Amen

## REFLECTION

- What is God promising you today?
- Where are you?
- Is anything in your life pushing God from first place?
- Where do you need assurance that you have enough?
- Where do you find it difficult to find God?
- Have you experienced fullness of joy?

## GOD'S CALLING CARD

# 4

# **Moses and the Burning Bush**
(Exodus 3; 4)

*When the LORD saw that he had gone over to look, God called to him from within the bush, 'Moses! Moses!'*

Exodus 3:4

At the end of a church service one Sunday evening, a man stopped me as I left. 'Will you share your story next week?' In a flash, I thought about what that would mean. Standing up in front of people. Bad plan. Spotlights and I are not great friends. Speaking, when I couldn't hear what I was saying. Bad plan. What if I spoke too loudly, or too quietly, or mumbled, or tripped over my words? Remembering what to say. Bad plan. Memory is not my strong point. I couldn't share my story. I opened my mouth to tell the man so. And found myself saying 'yes' . . .

Today started just like any other day, really. Me, in the desert, looking after my father-in-law's sheep. I led the sheep towards Mount Horeb, and that's when the day stopped being normal. I saw a bush on fire. That's not unusual in the desert. It's so hot, and bushes do catch fire. What was strange about this one, though, was that the bush didn't burn up. Later, I realized that it was the angel of the Lord appearing to me in flames, but I didn't know that at the time. I went closer, to check out why the bush wasn't burning up. God saw me going to look, and called to me from the bush . . .

Close enough to call.

'Moses! Moses!' and I answered, 'Here I am.'

Here I am. Again. How would you answer now? Where's your 'here'? Maybe different from yesterday. Or an hour ago. Keep answering the echo from Eden:
**Where are you?**
Here I am.

The bush was on fire, but it didn't burn up.
The outside was ablaze, hot, not looking very bush-like at all. But the inside, the bush itself, did not burn up. Surrounded by fire, it was fine.

> *For God, who said, 'Let light shine out of darkness,' made his light shine in our hearts to give us the light of the knowledge of God's glory displayed in the face of Christ. But we have this treasure in jars of clay to show that this all-surpassing power is from God and not from us.*
>
> 2 Corinthians 4:6,7

Jars of clay.
Sometimes we feel overwhelmed by flames that hit us. Health problems, work problems, family problems. From

the outside, things don't look good. We are like jars of clay.
Often damaged.
But we have light shining in our hearts.
God's light.
Surrounded by fire, we are fine.
Or we can be.

*Therefore we do not lose heart. Though outwardly we
are wasting away, yet inwardly we are being renewed
day by day.*

2 Corinthians 4:16

And that outward wasting away, that jar of clay in which
we live, shows that we don't do things in our own strength.
We have a God who lives in us and enables us.
Day by day.

Father God
Thank you for renewing me.
Amen

The bush was on fire, but it was not consumed.

*Because of the LORD's great love we are not consumed,
for his compassions never fail.*

Lamentations 3:22

Horeb was the mountain of God. As Moses went in that
direction, he saw the burning bush. When he went closer
to look, that's when God called.
Moses had positioned himself in a place where God was.

And God called.

We have a God who can break into any situation. God could have called Moses when Moses was far away from Horeb.

But we also have a God who likes it when we draw near.

*Come near to God and he will come near to you.*

James 4:8

Father God

I want to be where you are.

Amen

Did you know that? God likes it when he sees you coming!

Luke 15 paints a picture of two men.

One watching. One worrying.

One waiting. One walking.

One welcoming. One welcomed.

'Where's my son?' thinks the father.

His eyes strain into the distance.

'My father won't want me,' thinks the son.

His faltering footsteps take him closer.

'Is that him, coming towards me?' wonders the father.

His eyes strain into the distance.

'I'm scared to go on,' thinks the son. 'But I don't want to turn back.'

His faltering footsteps take him closer.

And then there is no distance left to strain into. No footsteps left to take.

They're together.
Welcoming and welcomed.

The son, though far from perfect, was heading in the right direction.
Closer to his father.

We need to go close to our Father.
Head in the right direction.
And God says, **Welcome home.**
Always.

Father God
Thank you for welcoming me.
Amen

Since losing my hearing, my primary way of communicating with people is through lip-reading. Lip-reading is not an exact science and I often make mistakes, but one thing always holds true: if the person I am trying to lip-read is too far away from me, then however familiar I am with their lip pattern, I will not be able to understand what they are saying. They're not close enough for me to see.
But, when they are close enough, I can watch their lips. And the more I do, the more familiar I become with their lip pattern. And the more I understand what they are saying.

People often say, 'God doesn't speak to me.' I imagine we've all felt that way sometimes, that heaven is silent. Head in the right direction. Stay close. And keep focused on him.

I didn't just suddenly know how to lip-read when I lost my hearing. I had to work at it. Actually being deaf helped, though. It gave me extra incentive to try to make sense of the patterns made by other people's lips as they spoke. It was the only way they'd be able to speak to me. Yes, they could write things down, which was – and is – good and helpful, but sometimes I want more. I want the person to speak to me. And I want to be able to understand.

When we begin to follow Jesus, we won't necessarily be able to hear from him straight away. But we do have an incentive to work at it.

*For God speaks again and again, though people do not recognize it.*

Job 33:14, NLT

God speaks, and we want to learn to understand what he is saying.

Draw close to him,

focus on him,

and learn to recognize his voice.

Father God

I need to hear your voice.

Amen

Heaven can seem especially silent when we are going through difficult times. Where's God?

Well, what do we know?

Job certainly went through hard times. His livelihood, his home, his family, his health; all these were snatched from him. Did he find that hard? Yes. And he said so. Which is fine; it's important to acknowledge that life is tough sometimes. We are not called to pretend that everything is wonderful all the time.

In the midst of his loss, of his pain, of his suffering, Job basically said, 'This is hard.'

But what else did Job say?

> *I know that my redeemer lives, and that in the end he will stand on the earth.*
> *And after my skin has been destroyed, yet in my flesh I will see God.*
>
>                                               Job 19:25,26

*Life is terrible right now, but I still know what I know.*
*I know that Jesus is alive.*
Living God.
*I know that he will come back.*
Redeeming God.
*I know that I will see him.*
Real hope.
*I know.*

Father God
I know what I know.
Amen

'Do not come any closer,' said God . . .

Stop. Don't come any closer.
Just stop.
And be aware of his presence.

> *Be still, and know that I am God.*
>                         Psalm 46:10

This is quite a familiar verse. We can rattle it off. But, especially in the busyness of life, how do we move beyond 'rattling it off' as we dash from one thing to another, one worry to the next?
How can we make this verse doable?
How can we actually find stillness?
What if we reverse the verse?
**I am God.**
**You know that.**
**So be still.**
We can be still because we know that God is God.
And that is tremendously liberating.
He's in charge.
**I am God.**
**You know that.**
**So be still.**

God told me not to come any closer, but to take off my sandals and stay put. Because I was standing on holy ground.

The ground was holy and sacred because the presence of God was there.
So there's Moses, standing on holy ground.

He's stopped, just as God told him to.
But that's not enough.

There was something between Moses and the holy
ground. His shoes. And God said:
**Take them off.**
**They're getting in the way.**
**Getting in the way of you and holy ground.**

What gets in the way of you and God?
Not necessarily bad things in themselves. But good
things can become unhelpful if they are allowed to get in
the way of our spiritual lives.

I once bought some red shoes. Nothing wrong with
that, unless of course you don't like red.
My shoes were beautiful. They fitted perfectly. But I
couldn't walk in them. They had heels. I knew my balance
was not good, nor was my ankle strength, yet I bought the
shoes anyway. Because maybe I'd be able to walk in them.
In reality, they made me fall over. Now, I'm sure many
other people bought a pair of those shoes. And I expect
most could wear them without a problem. Those people
would probably have hardly given their shoes a second
thought as they carried on with their lives. Yet, for me, the
shoes came between me and life. They tripped me up and
made me fall.

We are all different. Things affect us differently. What
has a detrimental effect on my spiritual life may or may
not have the same effect on yours.

*Examine yourselves to see whether you are in the faith;
test yourselves. Do you not realise that Christ Jesus is in
you . . .?*

2 Corinthians 13:5

Don't let anything come between you and God.

*Worship the LORD in the splendour of his holiness.*
Psalm 96:9

Holy is where God is.
Is where God is where you want to be?

'I am the God of your father, the God of Abraham, the God of
Isaac and the God of Jacob.'²
When I heard that, I was really scared. I looked down and tried to
hide. I was afraid to look at God.

God hasn't said anything yet, beyond introducing himself.
He's simply said who he is, and Moses is awestruck. Often,
we – rightly – say things like: 'God did such and such for
me; isn't he amazing?'
How often do we say, 'God is God; isn't he amazing?'
Not because of what he's done, but because of who he is.

*The Son is the image of the invisible God . . . all things
have been created through him and for him. He is before
all things, and in him all things hold together.*
Colossians 1:15–17

Isn't God awe-strikingly amazing?

Father God
You are amazing.
Amen

God went on to tell me that he was aware of how miserable it is for the Israelites (my people) in Egypt. They work night and day as slaves, and are cruelly punished. God said he is going to rescue the people. What great news! In fact, he said, 'I have come down to rescue them'[3] because he is concerned about their suffering.

'I have come down to rescue them.'
Let's think about that. God came down. God still comes down. He's so much bigger than us, and yet, in Jesus, he comes down to where we are.

*For to us [each one of us] a child is born . . .*
Isaiah 9:6

Wherever we are. He comes.

*God has said, 'Never will I leave you; never will I forsake you.'*
Hebrews 13:5

The compassionate heart of God.
What does rescue from suffering look like?
Perhaps our automatic response to that question would be *no pain, or difficulty, or struggle,* and maybe it's true for some people. We certainly have a God who can, and does, heal people, from all sorts of things. Which is wonderful.

But what about when he doesn't? When every day includes the experience and knowledge that no, I haven't been healed.

Paul had a thorn in the flesh. What the problem was, we don't know. What we do know is that he begged God to take it away. Three times he pleaded with God to rescue him from suffering. And God said 'no'.

> *But [God] said to me, 'My grace is sufficient for you, for my power is made perfect in weakness.'*
>
> 2 Corinthians 12:9

'But.' Not being healed wasn't the end.
'My grace is sufficient for you.' **You can do this. You can live the life you have. Because of grace. My grace. Sufficient for you. Not someone else. You. In your situation. My you-shaped, tailor-made grace.**
'My power is made perfect in weakness.'
When we are weak in ourselves, we can know a power not our own.
Not rescue from suffering, but rescue in suffering.

> *Be content with what you have, because God has said,*
> *'Never will I leave you;*
> *never will I forsake you.'*
>
> Hebrews 13:5

Be content with what you have.
**I will never leave you.**

You have God with you.
**My grace is sufficient for you.**
You have his grace-promise with you.
**Be content with what you have.**

> *I have learned to be content whatever the circumstances.*
> *I know what it is to be in need, and I know what it is*
> *to have plenty. I have learned the secret of being content*
> *in any and every situation, whether well fed or hungry,*
> *whether living in plenty or in want. I can do all this*
> *through him who gives me strength.*
>
> Philippians 4:11–13

We have treasure in jars of clay. So often, we focus on the jars of clay.[4] On our weaknesses. On the things which seem to work out for other people but never for us.
Let's focus on the treasure.
God's light shining in our hearts.

Father God
I want to learn to be content whatever my
circumstances.
I can learn the secret through you, who give me strength.
I can learn it through focusing on treasure.
Your light, shining in my heart.
Amen

As God carried on talking, the realization dawned on me. He wanted to use me to rescue his people. He wanted me to go to talk to the elders; me to go and talk to the king. Me! How can I talk eloquently to the king? I stutter, for one thing. I think it's a great plan to rescue God's people, but someone else should do it. Not me.

It's a great plan if someone else does it.
But God says: **No**. **It's a great plan if you do it.**
The Christian life is about bringing ourselves back, again and again, into God's agenda. And sometimes it is difficult to do that. Like Moses, we say, 'I can't do this.'
And we argue.
'No, God, it's not a good idea to use me for this. I'll mess up. I'll get it wrong.'
We focus on what we aren't, not on what we are.

What you aren't is known by God.
He made you.
What you are is known by God.
He made you.
If God says you can do something,
you can do it.

Moses focused on his weakness, not on God's strength. And so his weakness became greater to him than the God who just happened to be speaking to him from a burning bush. Put like that, it might seem a bit strange. God is able to speak from a burning bush, actually *is* speaking from a burning bush, and yet Moses doubts. He takes his eyes off the One who is speaking, and looks at himself. He sees his weaknesses, and they terrify him. Terror which stops him from seeing them in the light of God's power.
'I can do all this through him who gives me strength.'

So can you.
Whatever 'this' is.

Father God
Help me to see my weakness as opportunity
for your strength.
Amen

I asked God to send someone else. He was really cross with me for that. He said no, I was going, he'd chosen me to do it. But he said my brother would help me. It's still scary, but I'll find it better knowing I have Aaron with me.

Moses basically said, 'Let someone else do it.' He focused on his 'can'ts'.
What about us?
Do you focus on your can'ts, not your 'cans'?
What about in our lives, churches, day-to-day. It can be easy to sit back and let someone else do things. But is that what God is asking?
He won't ask everyone to do everything, but he'll ask everyone to do something.
Be it stand up and preach, be it serve coffee, be it lead worship, be it draw alongside someone who is lonely . . .
We are part of the body of Christ.

> *In Christ we, though many, form one body, and each*
> *member belongs to all the others.*
>
> Romans 12:5

Fellowship and sharing and supporting each other is important.

*'I can do things you cannot, you can do things I cannot; together we can do great things.'*

Attributed to Mother Teresa[5]

God called into Moses' curiosity. Into his 'What's going on?' when he experienced something he didn't understand. It's OK to be curious. It's OK to ask, 'What's going on here?' Moses went over to see why the bush did not burn up. And that's the last mention of the 'strange sight'[6] he didn't understand. The answer was 'God was there'.

And that was enough.

God clothed Moses in ability. Ability to believe that, in God, he was able.

*Now to him who is able to do immeasurably more than all we ask or imagine, according to his power that is at work within us, to him be glory in the church and in Christ Jesus throughout all generations, for ever and ever! Amen.*

Ephesians 3:20,21

*Higher than the heavens,*
*you come down.*
*Down to this world.*
*Down to where we are.*
*Down to where I am.*
*And where I am is a long way down.*
*The ground beneath my feet crumbles*
*and I slip further*
*and further.*
*Yet you're there.*

*Always.*
*However low I go,*
*you're there.*
*'I can't do it any more,'*
*I whisper.*
**Thank you,**
*you say.*
*My pain and tear-filled eyes ask questions.*
*'Thank you?'*
**Thank you for allowing me to perfect my strength in you.**
*But I said I can't do it any more.*
*I can't cope.*
*I'm not strong.*
**My child, you are never stronger than when you turn to me and say, 'I can't'.**

> *[God says to me] 'My grace is sufficient for you, for my power is made perfect in weakness.'*
>
> 2 Corinthians 12:9

Father God
To me, a child is born.
Thank you for entering my world,
bringing strength
and grace
and holiness.
Help me to take off my shoes.
I will be still
and know
you are God.
Amen

## REFLECTION

- What does your jar of clay look like? Remind yourself that God's light is inside it.
- How does God speak to you?
- What gets in the way of you and God?
- How much do you value the body of Christ?
- Write five things about who God is. Thank him for them.

## GOD'S CALLING CARD

# 5

# Moses Up the Mountain
(Exodus 19)

*Then Moses went up to God, and the LORD called to him from the mountain.*

v. 3

My sister is a traveller. She loves nothing more than taking holidays and minibreaks. She travels the world over, with one basic rule: not to go and visit somewhere she's already been.

Once, she'd booked a holiday, and then I ended up having an operation and spent weeks in hospital. This need not have affected my sister's plans. She could have jetted away and ticked another place off her list. But she decided to tick 'ward 15' off her list instead. She cancelled her holiday and camped out by my hospital bed.

I'm back at the mountain. To cut a long story short (you can read the whole story in Exodus), eventually the king did let us leave Egypt. It happened three months ago and today we came to the desert. I have never been so thankful for all those years I spent in this very desert, looking after sheep. I know my way around it quite well.

Moses' past helped shape who God called him to be in the present. He'd looked after sheep in the desert where God now wanted him to look after and shepherd his people.

In Mark 14, Peter, one of Jesus' closest friends, denies that he knows Jesus. Three times, when asked, he answers, 'I don't even know the man.'

Fast forward to John 21. A lot has happened since Peter's denials. Jesus has died on a cross, been buried, and is alive again.

Peter and Jesus are walking together on a beach, deep in conversation. The conversation is about love.

Jesus asks, 'Peter, do you love me?'

'Yes,' says Peter. 'You know I do.'

'Feed my lambs.'

They walk on.

'Peter, do you love me?'

'Yes. You know I do.'

'Take care of my sheep.'

They walk on.

'Peter, do you love me?'

'You know that I love you.'

'Feed my sheep.'

Three times Jesus asked Peter. Peter had denied knowing him three times.

And Peter goes on to become a shepherd of the flock that is the church.

Like Moses, Peter's past helped shape who God was calling him to be now.

A shepherd and overseer. Equipped to shepherd the church, in all its humanness, because he'd been there. Peter knew what it was like to hit rock bottom. He was distraught following his denials of Jesus. And he knew what it was like to have Jesus lift him up. He even wrote about it:

> *Humble yourselves, therefore, under God's mighty hand, that he may lift you up in due time.*
>
> 1 Peter 5:6

## Peter, do you love me? Right now?

Now is what matters.

Sometimes we can try to hide negative aspects of ourselves from other people and from God. Times we mess up, or say the wrong thing, or don't do things we should. Or we become so consumed with remorse, that everything we do, we do with the shadow of our past hanging over us.

Peter's story is in the Bible for a reason. Redemption is possible. Imagine if his story skipped straight to the 'yes, I love you' part. Wouldn't we miss so much? Wouldn't the church Peter went on to shepherd have missed out on so much?

Missed out on the part that says, nothing is bad enough to make God turn his back on you.
Missed out on the part that says, you're still worth it.
Missed out on the part that says, God can still use you.

Father God
Help me to be real.
Amen

Did Peter wish he hadn't denied Jesus? Probably. But his denial was used for good.

Until I was 21 years old, I could hear. Now I am deaf, a question I am asked frequently is whether I wish I'd been born deaf. In other words, whether I'd prefer never to have known what hearing is like.

The answer is 'no'. Painful though it is to know what I no longer have, I couldn't live the life I now live without that knowledge. For one thing, had I been born deaf, the chances are I'd find it difficult to talk, never having heard speech in order to learn. And yet now, I speak a lot. Public speaking in various settings is something I am privileged to do.

Could Peter have lived the life he went on to live, leading a church, had he not denied Jesus? We don't know. But we do know that Moses and Peter both had pasts that served as training grounds for their futures. Pasts that would enable them both to lead and empathize with the flocks they were called to shepherd.

> *Be shepherds of God's flock that is under your care, watching over them – not because you must, but because you are willing, as God wants you to be.*
>
> 1 Peter 5:2

Jesus doesn't say to Peter 'I love you', though he does love Peter.

*For I am convinced that neither death nor life, neither angels nor demons, neither the present nor the future, nor any powers, neither height nor depth, nor anything else in all creation, will be able to separate us from the love of God that is in Christ Jesus our Lord.*

Romans 8:38,39

You are loved. Full stop.

Jesus says, 'Peter, do you love me?' In other words, **I still want your love.**
**Do I have it? Do you love me?**
Whatever we do, or say, or feel, our love is precious to him. That's why he died.
**Beloved, do you love me?**

> Father God
> I love you.
> Amen

We all set up camp at the bottom of the mountain. When everyone was settled, more or less, I left them and climbed up the mountain.

They set up camp at the bottom of the mountain.
The mountain was Sinai (or Horeb), the 'mountain of God'.
When people set up camp, it literally means they are readying a place for sleeping outdoors.
So, the people prepared to rest by the mountain of God.
Where do you rest?

*My soul, find rest in God; my hope comes from him.*
                                        Psalm 62:5

Do you make a deliberate choice to go to God and rest?
Let him lead you there.
Be still.

| | |
|---|---|
| *The LORD is my shepherd, I lack nothing.* | I have all I need. |
| *He makes me lie down in green pastures,* | He lets me stop, |
| *he leads me beside quiet waters,* | he takes me to peaceful places, |
| *he refreshes my soul.* | he gives me strength for every 'now'. |

                                        Psalm 23:1–3

In 1 Kings 17, we read that Elijah's life is in danger. He's on the run. At one point, he collapsed in the desert and prayed that he would die. But God strengthened him and he carried on. Day after day, until he reached Horeb. The mountain of God. When he got there, he stopped. He spent the night in a cave. In a sense, he too set up camp at the mountain of God. He rested. And here's the thing: God let him.

God let him stay, rest, sleep in the mountain of God.
God lets us stay, rest, sleep in his presence.
We don't have to be 'doing' in his presence all the time.

God did speak to Elijah, but not until the night was over and he'd rested.

Sometimes, just resting in an awareness of God is enough.
Just being where he is.
And, when the time is right, he'll speak.
Just as he spoke to Elijah.

The Elijah who arrived was travel-weary.
And God came to him in a gentle whisper.
Maybe you arrive travel-weary.
Tired from life.
That's OK.
Let the God of all compassion come to you in gentleness,
in quietness, in a whisper that's just for you.

**Come to me. You are weary and burdened. I will give you rest.**[1]

Let his whisper echo in you: **Beloved, I'm here. Just be still.**

> Father God
> I am your beloved.
> Amen

Up I went, climbing higher and higher up the mountain. And then I heard the voice of God, calling to me.

Close enough to call.

God told me what to say to the people at the bottom of the mountain.

*You yourselves have seen what I did to Egypt, and how
I carried you on eagles' wings and brought you to myself.
Now if you obey me fully and keep my covenant, then
out of all nations you will be my treasured possession.*

Exodus 19:4,5

God said to the people, 'You . . . have seen what I did.'
We have a living God. He's always doing.

'You . . . have seen what I did.'
**You've lived through some amazing times with me.
Don't forget them.**
'You . . . have seen what I did.'

Have you? Have you seen what God's doing? Have you
looked?
If you don't look, you won't see.
In every day, there is something to be thankful for. Something God's put there, for you to see. Something he's done.

I decided to look for things to be thankful for on the day
I was told I'd lose my hearing. As I walked out of the hospital, I was feeling the opposite of thankful, and it was
raining. Then I saw a rainbow. A bright spot in the rain.
And I decided to look for 'rainbows' to be thankful for,
every day.
At first, I would be thankful for someone giving me directions, or opening a door for me. Things like that. And,
gradually, those things became thankfulness to God for
putting someone there who could give me directions.

And, as I recognized him in more and more places, I began to see what he is doing. Every day, he's busy doing things. All around.

Have a look.

And see.

What's God doing where you are?

Father God
Help me see.
Amen

The Israelites were stuck in Egypt. Day after day, slavery was all they knew. They longed to escape, but didn't know how. They couldn't see a way out. And God stepped in. Through miracles and signs and wonders that could only come from God, he set them free.

*It is for freedom that Christ has set us free. Stand firm, then, and do not let yourselves be burdened again by a yoke of slavery.*

Galatians 5:1

Did you know you've been set free?

Free from slavery to guilt, to regret, to striving, to never feeling good enough.

Jesus Christ came, and died on the cross, and rose again, to set you free.

Did he do it so you'd be free to be crushed under the weight of whispers – from the world and yourself – 'you're never going to match up'?

No. He did it so you'd be free to know freedom.

Free to know that you don't need to be perfect, or feel guilty all the time.

You are free from all that!

Free to know that you are loved.

And that nothing can undo that love.

'I carried you on eagles' wings and brought you to myself . . .'

**I carried you.**

**I brought you to me.**

**I did it.**

**You're not here by chance.**

**You're not in my presence by some sort of fluke.**

**You're here because I want you to be.**

**Know the freedom of being lifted in the midst of life.**

**Relax.**

**I've got you.**

**I won't let you fall.**

> *He will cover you with his feathers, and under his wings you will find refuge.*
>
> Psalm 91:4

'. . . you will be my treasured possession.'

The Hebrew for 'treasured possession' refers to belonging.

We are redeemed by God.

Bought and brought back by him.

Treasure.

*Do not fear, for I have redeemed you;*
*I have summoned you by name; you are mine.*
*When you pass through the waters, I will be with you;*
*and when you pass through the rivers, they will not*
*sweep over you.*
*When you walk through the fire, you will not be burned;*
*the flames will not set you ablaze.*
*For I am the* LORD *your God, the Holy One of Israel,*
*your Saviour;*
*I give Egypt for your ransom, Cush and Seba in your*
*stead.*
*Since you are precious and honoured in my sight, and*
*because I love you . . .*

Isaiah 43:1–4


Father God
I don't feel like treasure.
Yet I am treasure to you.
Amen


I 'brought you to myself'.

In reminding them of who he was, and all he'd done, and who they were, or could be, in him, God called into the people's forgetting.

One of the most common things found in supermarket lost property, apparently, is walking sticks. People put their sticks down as they reach for a tin of beans, put the tin in their trolley, and walk away. It's easy to do; I've done it myself.

It's when I exit the supermarket and leave the trolley behind that I notice. I notice I'm struggling to walk, because I've not got my stick.

Sometimes our struggling can be a reminder that we've forgotten to bring God along, to help.

Using a stick doesn't mean I can walk perfectly. But it does mean I have support.

Having God with us doesn't mean life will be easy. But it does mean we are not alone. He's with us.

'I carried you on eagles' wings and brought you to myself . . .'

**Don't forget what I did.**

**What I do.**

God called into their forgetting and clothed them in remembrance.

Remembrance of who he was.

And who they were to him.

**You're my treasured possession.**

**Beloved, do you love me?**


*I walk with Jesus on the beach that is my life.*
*The waves come and go on the shore.*
*We walk together, Jesus and I.*
*We reach the point in my life I'd rather forget.*
*The lowest point.*
*The time – or one of the times – I messed up.*
*He turns to me.*
*I wait for words of warning.*
*Chastising.*
*Rebuke.*

*Or disappointment.*
*He must be disappointed in me.*
**Do you love me?**
*What, no mention of all I haven't done?*
*My eyes search his face.*
*He looks straight back at me.*
*Calmly waiting.*
**Do you love me?**
*The words echo through me.*
*I want to say 'yes', but I can't.*
*Not because I don't love him.*
*But because I'm in the wrong place.*
*Why would he want my love from the rubbish*
*and stress*
*and frustration*
*and anger*
*on this section of the beach that is my life?*
*That is me?*
*We stand together, Jesus and I.*
*The waves come and go on the shore.*
*I look ahead.*
*Not far away is a good time.*
*Everything was going well.*
*If I can just get to that place, he'll want my love more from*
*there.*
*I'm sure of it.*
**Do you love me?**
*'Come on!'*
*I urge him to hurry.*

*Hurry to the place where I'm doing well,*
*so I can tell him I love him.*
*He stands still.*
*In the middle of my rubbish.*
*He knows where he is.*
*I know he knows.*
*Looking at me, he asks again:*
**Do you love me?**
*Surrounded by my rubbish,*
*I say, 'Yes.*
*I love you.'*
*His smile says it all.*
*He loves me, too.*
*I walk with Jesus on the beach that is my life.*
*The waves come and go on the shore.*
*We walk together, Jesus and I.*

*I am my beloved's and my beloved is mine.*

Song of Songs 6:3

Father God
Sometimes, I forget to look.
So I don't see.
I don't see all the ways you show your presence.
I don't see the way you look after me.
Help me look for rainbows.
You put them there for me to see.
Help me not to miss them.
Amen

**REFLECTION**

- Do you love Jesus right now?
- Where do you need to find rest?
- What is God doing in your life at the moment?
- What do you need to remember about God, every day? Stick it on your bathroom mirror.
- What part of God's flock is under your care? Think of names. And then pray for them.

**GOD'S CALLING CARD**

# 6

# Moses and the Cloud
(Exodus 24)

 *On the seventh day the LORD called to Moses from within the cloud.*

v. 16

I sat, story book in hand, my niece cuddled in beside me. I was reading the book to her. It was a gripping story and she was engrossed. Then she started wriggling a bit. 'Abbie?' I asked. 'Are you alright?' Fervent nod of her little head. I carried on reading, she carried on wriggling. In the end, I said, 'Abbie, what's the matter?' A desperate look came over her face. 'I need to go to the bathroom, but I don't want to miss the story!' I took her hand in mine and, together, we pressed an imaginary pause button. When Abbie got back, we pressed 'play'. We carried on with the story, and she hadn't missed any of it.

God has just made a covenant with us. An agreement between us and him that he will be our God and we will be his people. Then he told me to go with the leaders of Israel up the mountain to him. After we'd worshipped together, I was to go and approach God on my own.[1]

Communal worship was important. It still is. Something special happens when we meet as followers of Jesus. We encourage each other, share together, are reminded that we belong to the family of God.

> *Let us consider how we may spur one another on towards love and good deeds, not giving up meeting together, as some are in the habit of doing, but encouraging one another.*

Hebrews 10:24,25

'Meeting together' can involve thousands and it can involve a few.

> *For where two or three gather in my name, there am I with them.*

Matthew 18:20

The important thing is that we have people to meet with. People to journey with, through the ups and downs, people we can encourage and be encouraged by.
Do you have people like that?

Father God
Thank you for people who encourage me.
Amen

But communal worship and relationship should not replace individual relationship with God. It can't. Yet, sometimes, our spiritual lives can become defined through the spiritual lives of others. *They're doing fine, I'm spending time with them, so I must be doing fine, too.* Not necessarily . . .

In Mark 8:27–30, Jesus is with his disciples. They are chatting, and Jesus asks the group, 'Who do people say I am?' They replied that there were various opinions. John the Baptist; Elijah; one of the prophets.

The disciples knew what people around them were saying about Jesus. They were engaged enough to know.

It's important that we engage with the world around us, know what people are saying, know where their thinking is coming from. After all, Jesus asked his disciples about others; he clearly expected them to know.

The same can apply in our lives. 'Who do people say Jesus is?' Are we talking about him? Or do we tend to talk about life in general to the exclusion of spiritual life?

'Who do people say I am?'

Who is God to your neighbour, or your friend, or the person who sits on the third row from the front at church? Why not ask them?

Then comes a 'But' from Jesus.

'But what about you? . . . Who do you say I am?'

**What about you? You matter.**

**You.**

Who is God to you? How would you answer that question?

Father God

To me, right now, you are . . .

Amen

Things change. Circumstances change. People change.
But God never changes.
'I AM WHO I AM.'[2]
In everything.

> *One God and Father of all, who is over all and through all and in all.*

Ephesians 4:6

Peter answers Jesus. 'You are the Messiah.'[3] Or in Matthew 16:16: 'You are the Christ, the Son of the Living God.' And Jesus says to Peter, 'Good. You didn't learn this from people; my Father in heaven has shown it to you.'

There comes a point in our spiritual lives when, perhaps guided and prompted by things others say, we need to take responsibility for our own walk with God.

Matthew 7
Two men.
Both builders.
Two foundations.
One rock, one sand.
Two houses.
Stormy weather.
One house.

The men were different. The houses they built were probably different. The foundations they chose were different. But both houses looked fine. Until bad weather.

When the storms came, only the house on the rock was able to stand. The other house collapsed. It had nothing firm to hold on to.

The men were responsible for choosing their foundations. One got it right. One got it wrong.

Choose God as your life foundation.

And you'll get it right.

> *My God is my rock.*
> 2 Samuel 22:3

Father God
Help me build my life on you.
Amen

So we went and worshipped together and, as we did, we saw the God of Israel! It was awesome. It's hard to describe it. Under God's feet was something like a pavement made of sapphire. So clear. We saw God. And then we ate and drank. Nothing bad happened.

They saw God.

I remember doing a Bible study on the Beatitudes (Matt. 5), and one of the questions was: 'Which is your favourite Beatitude?' Which, in the list, especially draws you?

How to choose one? They are all so profound, so beautiful, so important.

> *Blessed are the poor in spirit, for theirs is the kingdom of heaven.*

*Blessed are those who mourn, for they will be comforted.*
*Blessed are the meek, for they will inherit the earth.*
*Blessed are those who hunger and thirst for righteousness,*
*for they will be filled.*
*Blessed are the merciful, for they will be shown mercy.*
*Blessed are the pure in heart, for they will see God.*
*Blessed are the peacemakers, for they will be called chil-*
*dren of God.*
*Blessed are those who are persecuted because of righteous-*
*ness, for theirs is the kingdom of heaven.*

Matthew 5:3–10

Which would you choose?

The one I chose was: 'Blessed are the pure in heart, for they will see God.'

To see God. Not what he's doing, or what he did, or what he will do, but to see him.

It's no accident that it was as Moses and the others worshipped that they saw God. True worship produces a purity in our hearts. As we worship, we make room in our hearts to see God.

What about if worship is not confined to communal times of singing? These times are vital, but our worship doesn't need to end when they do.

If we can learn to live in a constant state of worship, to offer our lives as worship to God, we will see him more and more.

As we worship, expressing our awe of our amazing God, we very often find ourselves breaking out into praise, expressing our thanks to him.

But sometimes it is hard.

> *Praise the LORD, my soul; all my inmost being, praise his holy name.*
>
> Psalm 103:1

I have struggled with this verse. The 'all my inmost being' part gets me stumped.

Inmost being. Inner parts. My inmost being is riddled with tumours. How can praise come from them?

> *Though the fig-tree does not bud and there are no grapes on the vines, though the olive crop fails and the fields produce no food, though there are no sheep in the sheepfold and no cattle in the stalls, yet I will rejoice in the LORD, I will be joyful in God my Saviour.*
>
> Habakkuk 3:17,18

The Hebrew translated as 'inmost being' doesn't simply mean physical inner being. It extends to heart and mind, thoughts and feelings.

I will make a deliberate choice to rejoice in God. Despite everything, I will find something good. Something I can thank him for. Something I can praise him for.

I will.

Saying 'I will' like that is worship. Expressing reverence to our unchangeable God, even though the fig tree does not blossom. When we do that – when we come to God in our tears, in our pain, in our confusion, and in them (even through them) manage to whisper, 'I will rejoice in you,' – we see him.

And as we let him into our hearts, those cracked and bruised and hurting hearts, he purifies them by his presence.

'Blessed are the pure in heart, for they will see God.'

Father God
I will rejoice in you.
Amen

After Moses and the others had seen God, what did they do? They ate and drank. They carried on with life.

The 'mountain top' experience, the overwhelming feel of God's presence, did not last forever. Realistically, mountain top experiences don't. Those times when we're riding high, feeling on top of the world, close to God, they come and go. We might want them to stay all the time, but they don't. At some point, we have to come down from the mountain and carry on with life.

Peter, James and John had a literal mountain top experience. It's described in Matthew 17.

They went up a mountain with Jesus. Just them and him. When they got to the top of the mountain, Jesus was transfigured. He shone. The disciples saw it. Moses and Elijah appeared. God's voice came from heaven. The disciples heard it.

And then it was time to go back down the mountain. Back to everyday life.

They probably would have liked to stay up the mountain with Jesus. But they had to come down.

So down they went.

Crucially, Jesus went with them.

At the bottom of the mountain, the disciples were faced with their own inability to understand, with their own inability to heal people, with weakness and struggles within themselves.

And Jesus was with them.

Jesus chose to come down to where the messiness of life was. And he chose to stay.

*Surely I am with you always, to the very end of the age.*
Matthew 28:20

Father God
Thank you that nothing in my life
will scare you away.
Amen

Then God told me to go further up the mountain to him. He said I'm to stay there, and he'll give me the commands he has written to show us how to live. Before I went, I asked the leaders to wait for me until I came back to them. I also told them that Aaron and Hur were in charge, and they'd look out for them. When I went up the mountain, cloud covered it, and the glory of the Lord settled on it. I stayed there, waiting, for six days.

The discipline of waiting. It's not an easy one. We all have times of waiting. Waiting for a train, or for an appointment, or for tomorrow . . .
Will we wait in our waiting?

To wait means to remain, or rest, expectantly.

> Father God
> Help me find release
> to rest in you as I wait.
> Amen

When we find ourselves remaining static, not sure what lies ahead, perhaps impatient, will we choose to wait in expectation? Expectation of what God will do?

> *But as for me, I watch in hope for the LORD, I wait for God my Saviour.*
>
> Micah 7:7

I watch in hope. I expect my God to come into my watching. And I believe he will. In his timing.
That's what waiting is. Watching for God, expecting God, trusting in God's timing.

> *But I trust in you, LORD; I say, 'You are my God.' My times are in your hands.*
>
> Psalm 31:14,15

We may think it's all very well for the psalmist to write this. Everything was probably fine for them. If they went through tough things like we do, it would have been a different story.

Well, let's just think about that. David, who wrote the psalm, was living with poor health, surrounded by enemies, and rejected even by his closest friends.

That's why verse 14 starts with the word 'but'. Despite all that is going on, I trust you.

The psalms are a great example to us of keeping things real. They don't pretend life is always easy. They do teach us how to find the 'trust-but'.

The but that enables us to trust, even in our darkest times. 'You are my God.'

You. Are. My. God.

When we go through bad times, we always have a choice. Will I go through this on my own, or will I go through it with God by my side?

Find the trust-but.

You. Are. My. God.

I choose to go through things with God. My times are in his hands. I don't know what my times will bring, and often when I find out, they are not times I'd choose. Another operation, another tumour, further rehabilitation. But I choose to remember that my times are in his hands.

Find the trust-but.

You. Are. My. God.

*For I am the LORD your God who takes hold of your*
*right hand and says to you,*
*Do not fear; I will help you.*

Isaiah 41:13

**I am God.**
**You know that.**
**So be still.**

> Father God
> Help me find trust-buts.
> You are my God.
> Amen

Moses knew he needed to go, and he put things in place. He made sure people knew what was happening and who was in charge. Aaron would look after the others.

How good are we at waiting with or for people?

When I was first diagnosed with Neurofibromatosis Type 2, things happened quite quickly. I was scanned, given medication, and told to stay in bed, doing as little as possible, while I waited for a date for brain surgery.

It was as I lay there that my mum came to tell me her plan. She would regularly write a letter/email/update about how things were going with me. She'd then send it out to family, friends, interested people, so that they could support us in thought or prayer.

I didn't want people knowing the details of my life, and I said 'no'. Mum persuaded me otherwise – as mums tend to – and I learned the privilege of having people wait with me. My waiting was prayed over, prayed into, shared.

By asking the leaders to wait for him, Moses was asking them to share in his situation.

*Rejoice with those who rejoice; mourn with those who mourn.*
Romans 12:15

In order to act on this verse, we need to be like Moses. We need to ask people to wait with us. Ask them to be in our situation. We need to tell people what our situation is, and allow them to share it.

Otherwise, not only do we miss out on having people wait with us, we prevent people from sharing our joys and sorrows.

*Carry each other's burdens, and in this way you will fulfil the law of Christ.*
Galatians 6:2

Father God
Help me to let others share my burdens.
Amen

On the seventh day, God called to me from inside the cloud.

Close enough to call.

Moses waited for six days. And then God spoke.
But God's silence for those six days did not mean he wasn't there. He was present the whole time. The 'glory of the LORD'[4] was there.
All around. Just as it always is.
God is always there, right with us, every second. Even in our waiting. Maybe especially in our waiting.

When God created the world, it was the seventh day on which he rested.[5]

He looked at all he'd made, saw that it was good, and rested. The seventh day was the day on which it was time to stop creating.

For Moses, the seventh day was the day on which it was time to stop waiting.

Time for God to speak.

God will speak.
In his timing.
Be patient.
You are my God.

> *Be still before the LORD and wait patiently for him.*
> Psalm 37:7

Father God
Be with me in my waiting.
Amen

I climbed further up the mountain, and I entered the cloud.

Wait for God.

God called into Moses' obedience. Moses was where God was, doing what God had told him to do, obeying. And still God called. Still God wanted to get his attention.

Sometimes, we can get caught up in a whirlwind of 'obedience' and forget that God still speaks. God is a living

God. A God at work. A God who doesn't get stuck in our routine.

But perhaps we do.

We go to church, attend a home group, help with the children's work, or serve the coffee, or lead worship. It all becomes automatic and we get so caught up in it that we forget to allow room for God to speak.

Those six days of waiting in God's presence would have prepared Moses' heart to hear God.

In the busyness of life, let's make sure we allow room for God to speak.

Time in his presence to just be.

Time to press pause, so we don't miss out on God's story.

Moses was close to God. And God clothed him in 'get closer'.

We can never be as close as we can be to God. Because he always calls us to grow closer.

How's your growing going?

*I am the vine; you are the branches.*

John 15:5

Think of a vine. Think of its branches. There's a point where the two merge, and it's impossible to see where the vine ends and the branch begins.

Get closer.

*I had a fig tree.*
*It blossomed.*
*I didn't rejoice in God.*

*But when my tree withered,*
*I found the trust-but.*
*And I rejoiced.*
*I had a good life.*
*Things were going well.*
*I didn't rejoice in God.*
*But when my life crumbled,*
*I found the trust-but.*
*And I rejoiced.*
*It wouldn't have been hard to rejoice*
*when the fig tree blossomed*
*and things were going well.*
*At least, I don't think it would.*
*I can't be sure.*
*Because I didn't try it.*

*Rejoice in the Lord always. I will say it again: rejoice!*
Philippians 4:4

Father God
Help me to pause.
As I wait in my waiting,
may I find you.
You are my God.
Closer than close.
My Rock.
My strong foundation.
Help me to remember I'm safe.
You know my future.
Please be with me in my waiting.
Amen

## REFLECTION

- Keep a list, every day for a week, of what God has been to you that day.
- What is your foundation? What do you look to for security?
- Where do you see God?
- What area of your life needs a trust-but?
- Can you share a burden with someone?

## GOD'S CALLING CARD

Grow closer

# 7

# **Samuel**
(1 Samuel 3)

 *Then the LORD called Samuel.*

v. 4

My niece, Elianne, started school when she was 3. When she was 2, she was determined that she was never going to school. 'I don't want to go to school.' And that was that. Then she turned 3, and everything changed. Not only did she get on board with the idea of going to school, she provided her parents with a verbal list of her requirements. 'School shoes (girl ones, not like my brother's), a skirt, a cardigan (red), a pink lunch box (with rainbow colours), sweets every day for a treat.' Notably absent from her list was 'whatever school say I need' . . .

I think something is wrong with Eli. He keeps calling me. It's happened three times now, and each time I've got out of bed and gone to see what he needs. But he says he didn't call me. I know he's getting old and now I'm worried that he is unwell. The third time was the strangest, though. Eli said if I hear the call again, I'm to answer: 'Speak, LORD, for your servant is listening.'¹ I don't even know the Lord.

'Know' here can mean recognize. Samuel didn't know or recognize God. And Eli pointed him in the right direction. Eli helped Samuel recognize God. What about us? Do we help people to know God? By what we say? By how we live? Eli means 'ascended, uplifted, high'.[2]

Eli wasn't perfect by any means. But he lived up to his name. Pointing people to God is one of the highest callings.

John the Baptist prepared people for Jesus' coming.
People flocked to John. He had something they wanted. He had good news. They needed to be baptized, and John baptized them. John constantly told them:
'Jesus is coming! Look out for him . . .'[3]
And then, Jesus came. He was there. The one they'd been waiting for. But some of John's friends/disciples weren't too sure. They were indignant that people were turning from John towards Jesus. And John said:

> *He must become greater; I must become less.*
> John 3:30

John wanted people to know Jesus. Not John. Jesus.
Much as Eli, who had been Samuel's teacher and mentor since Samuel was young, realized that Samuel needed to know God. Which meant Eli stepping back.

The difference between knowing about God and knowing God.
Have you moved from knowing about him to knowing him?

Father God
Help me to really know you.
Amen

Eli would still be there for Samuel but God himself needed to become greater in Samuel's life.
And how did that start?
Samuel said, 'Speak, Lord. I'm listening.'

In Exodus 33, we see Moses saying to God, 'I know I'm to lead these people, the Israelites. You've told me that. But you haven't told me who will be with me.'
God says, 'I will.'
**I will be with you.**
Just as God says to you, 'I will.'
Who will be with me in this life I'm living?
**I will be with you.**

Moses is a bit further on in his relationship with God than Samuel. Moses knows God, and he knows what God is asking him to do.
Samuel wonders: *Who* are you?
Answer? The Lord.
Moses wonders: *Where* are you?
Answer? With you.

> *Do not be afraid; do not be discouraged, for the LORD your God will be with you wherever you go.*
>
> Joshua 1:9

*Where are you?*
**I'm with you.**


Father God
Thank you that you are always with me.
Wherever I go.
Amen


After God says to Moses 'I will be with you', Moses says to God: 'Show me your glory.'[4]

Show me your glory. Remind me who you are and who is with me.
Moses is close to God.
But he still needs reminding.
It's good to remind ourselves that God is with us.
Always.
Faced with the responsibility of leading more than a million people, Moses could have said 'tell me what to do', 'tell me what's coming up', 'how long is this going to take'. But he didn't.
'Show me your glory.'
Show me more of you.


Father God
Show me your glory.
Amen


Sometimes, we come to God with a sort of spiritual shopping list. We know what we need, and if we show him our list, then, much like a shop assistant, he'll show us how to get it. Maybe he'll even fetch it for us.

What if what we actually need, rather than what we think we need, is simply – yet profoundly – more of God?

Show me your glory.

So here I am, lying in bed, waiting for a call. From someone I don't even know. Maybe the call won't come. Or what if I don't hear it properly?

> *The LORD came and stood there, calling as at the other times, 'Samuel! Samuel!'*
>
> 1 Samuel 3:10

Close enough to call.
Standing there.

> *The Lord stood at my side and gave me strength.*
>
> 2 Timothy 4:17

The Lord God.
Standing at your side.
Every day.
Giving you strength.
Every day.

I answered as Eli had told me to: 'Speak, LORD, for your servant is listening.'

Samuel invited God to speak. Then Samuel stopped talking.

When was the last time you said to God,

'Speak, I'm listening' and then waited?

Without your mind running here there and everywhere, or telling God what to say, or . . .

*Speak, Lord, I'm listening.*

Father God
Please speak;
I'm listening . . .
Amen

Eli taught Samuel to know God. He told Samuel what to say. And then stepped back and let Samuel learn it for himself.

Another of my nieces, Abbie, learned to say 'thank you' from a very young age. When given something: 'What do you say, Abbie?' 'Thank you.' Soon, she didn't need prompting. She'd learned when to say 'thank you'. One birthday, she asked for a doll to add to her collection of similar dolls. I had a look online, to choose one from the many available, and that's when I saw it. A doll who was deaf. The doll wore a little hearing aid device. I bought this doll who was deaf, wrapped it up, and watched Abbie open it on her birthday. She unwrapped the paper, pulled out the box containing a doll, smiled a 'thank you' when she saw it, and then set about taking the doll from the box. It wasn't until she'd done so that she saw the little aid on the doll's ear. She looked at it. Then she looked at me. Then she pushed the doll's hair back, to be sure she'd seen what she thought she'd seen. Her little face lit up. 'Her ears don't work; she's like you,' she said as she flew across the room and flung her arms around my neck. Truly a 'thank you' from the heart.

It was only because, time and time again, I or my sister have explained to Abbie about my hearing loss, that she was able to one day recognize it for herself. And, when she'd untangled herself from my neck, she picked up the doll, turned her to face me, and made her say 'thank you' in sign language. We've never taught her to make a doll do sign language, she learned that for herself.

How do we teach people to know God?

The Lord told me something really hard. He said he is going to punish Eli and his family, because they don't follow God's ways. Well, Eli does. But his sons don't, and Eli doesn't stop them. I lay back down until it was morning, then, as I always do, I opened the doors of God's house. I avoided Eli. I knew he'd want to know what had happened last night, but I was scared to tell him. In the end, though, Eli said 'Samuel!' and I knew I couldn't put it off any longer. I went to him, and said, 'Here I am.'[5]

Here I am. Again the echo. Where's your 'here' now?

Eli did ask me what the Lord had told me. He said, 'Don't keep anything back.' So I didn't. I told him everything. Eli listened and, when I'd finished, he just said, 'He is the LORD; let him do what is good in his eyes.'[6]

'He is the LORD; let him do what is good in his eyes.'
Eli, faced with difficult news, experienced release. Someone bigger than him was in the situation. God. And that is tremendously reassuring.

Often, when my scans show that one of my tumours has grown, there are options. The surgeon outlines them for me: operate, don't operate, operate from a certain angle, operate to debulk rather than remove the whole tumour, go in and take the whole tumour out, bearing in mind that will likely cause other nerve damage . . . the list goes on. And we discuss each option, the pros and cons. But, invariably, there comes a point where I say to the surgeon, 'What would you advise?'
I'm not a surgeon. I'm not equipped with the knowledge or experience to know which is the best option for me. So I ask someone who is. 'What would you advise?'

We are not equipped with the knowledge or experience of God. But God is.
'He is the LORD . . .'
In good times and bad, God is.
'. . . let him do what is good in his eyes.'

Job wrestled with what was going on in his life. He struggled with the bad things that were happening to him. Life was so hard. Health, livelihood, family had all vanished. Job wished he'd never been born.
Yet, through his wrestling, he concluded:

*I know that you can do all things; no purpose of yours
can be thwarted.
You asked, 'Who is this that obscures my plans without
knowledge?'
Surely I spoke of things I did not understand, things too
wonderful for me to know.*

Job 42:2,3,5

'He is the LORD; let him do what is good in his eyes.'

It's not our role to decide what is good in God's eyes. We
are not responsible for God's eyes.
But we are responsible for acknowledging their sovereignty.
For reaching a place, through – and within – our questioning that says, 'I'm not equipped with the knowledge of God.'

*My ears had heard of you but now my eyes have seen you.*
Job 42:5

The difference between knowing about God and knowing
God.

Father God
You are my God.
Amen

I was told I needed surgery which would very possibly ren-
der me unable to walk.
I wished I didn't need more surgery. What if I was left unable
to walk? What if something else went wrong? What if . . .?

In John 12:20–36, Jesus talks of his impending death. A painful, humiliating death on a cross. And that's hard. He finds it difficult. Crucially, Jesus doesn't pretend he doesn't find it difficult.

We don't need to pretend everything is OK if it's not.
That was good news for me as I faced surgery and possible paralysis. Everything was not OK.

Jesus says, 'Shall I ask my Father God to save me from this?'
God could have done it (see Matt. 26:53).
But no. 'It was for this very reason I came to this hour' (John 12:27).
There are many times in the Bible when people do ask God to spare them from things. Sometimes he says 'yes', sometimes he says 'no'. But it is certainly a legitimate prayer to pray. I've prayed it myself. I've wrestled with God. I've prayed, 'please, no more'.
On this occasion, though, Jesus' 'no' was helpful for me. Rather than praying 'save me from this' he prayed 'glorify your name' (v. 28).

What if I made that my prayer?
'Glorify your name.'
The longing of my heart, underneath all the struggles, and hurting, and wishing things were different, is that God gets the glory. Always.

So, before this operation, I prayed 'glorify your name'. I'd come through! I'd be able to walk just fine. And God would get the glory.

Then I read God's answer to Jesus' 'glorify your name' prayer.

'I have glorified it, and will glorify it again.'[7]

Has he glorified it in my life?

God has done amazing things in my life. The fact I am alive today is nothing short of miraculous. Everyone had given up hope when the team gathered to switch off my life support machine. Everyone, that is, except God. And yes, he's been given the glory. People have thanked him and praised him for what they've seen happen. Time and time again.

But surely to really be glorified this time, he'd heal me?

*Glorify your name. Make this operation work out just the way I want it to.*

**'Who is this that obscures my plans . . . without knowledge?'**[8]

*Um, I think it might be me.*

Who am I, to pray 'glorify your name' and then tell him how to do that?

I woke up from the surgery, and I couldn't walk.

Weeks later, my leg moved. Eventually, I was able to stand. To walk, aided by a frame. Then to walk aided by a stick.

During those long months in hospital, God was glorified through my struggles, not apart from them.

When I prayed with a fellow patient.

When a fellow patient prayed with me.

When we laughed and cried together.

God's glory shows up in unexpected places.

**'Who is this that obscures my plans . . . without knowledge?'**

'Glorify your name' is a bold prayer.

It is a vulnerable prayer.

It is saying, 'You're in charge.'

*I can do all this through him who gives me strength.*
Philippians 4:13

Give me the strength to pray 'glorify your name'.

Father God
Glorify your name.
Amen

In Genesis 32, we see that Jacob wrestled with God. And God blessed him in that wrestling.

It's OK to struggle with things God allows to come our way. OK to wrestle.

But, after the wrestling, as he walked on, Jacob was limping. A reminder to him that however strong he was in his own strength, God was stronger. God is God.

I still limp when I walk.

Like Jacob, I am constantly reminded, through my weakness, that God is in charge.

'He is the LORD; let him do what is good in his eyes.'

> *He says, 'Be still, and know that I am God;*
> *I will be exalted among the nations, I will be exalted in*
> *the earth.'*
>
> Psalm 46:10

**I am God.**
**You know that.**
**So be still.**

'He is the LORD; let him do what is good in his eyes.'

God called into Samuel's oblivion. Samuel was unaware
that the God he knew about was a God he could know.
Do you know the God you know about?
And God clothed Samuel in understanding.

> *You will seek me and find me when you seek me with all*
> *your heart.*
>
> Jeremiah 29:13

*My friend told me about God.*
*She said he's powerful.*
*So I filed it away under 'I know about God'.*
*My neighbour told me God is wise.*
*I filed that away, too.*
*I know about God.*
*Someone else told me God is caring.*
*I filed that away, too.*
*I know about God.*

*My list kept growing.*
*I kept reading it, learning it, memorizing it.*
*There's so much to know about God.*
*I'm sitting, waiting.*
*Waiting to see the doctor.*
*Waiting for my name to be called.*
*I open my file and remind myself.*
*I know about God.*
*He is powerful, wise, caring . . .*
*The list seems hollow today.*
*I don't know why.*
*I need more.*
*I ask the lady beside me to tell me something about God.*
*As she thinks about it, her name is called.*
*She stands, ready.*
*Ready to receive news about her illness.*
*Her symptoms have got worse, I know.*
*She told me.*
*Gathering her bags together, she says,*
*'Something I know about God?*
*He's here.'*
*I watch the door to the doctor's room close behind her.*
*He's here? With me? Right now?*
*I pick up my list, and cross out a word:*
*I know ~~about~~ God.*
*He's here.*

*I am with you and will watch over you wherever you go.*
Genesis 28:15

Father God
Help me to know you.
And, as I know you more,
to trust you more.
Really trust you.
In a way that says 'show me your glory',
and means it.
Please become greater in my life.
I invite you in.
More of you, less of me.
Glorify your name.
Amen

## REFLECTION

- Write five words which describe God to you.
- In what situation would you like to be reminded that God is with you?
- How do you feel about the idea of wrestling with God?
- Do you have a limp? Something which reminds you that God is stronger? Thank God for it.
- Write on a card 'God; glorify your name in me today' and stick it where you see it every morning/as you leave the house.


## GOD'S CALLING CARD

# 8

# Israel
(Hosea 11)

 *When Israel was a child, I loved him, and out of Egypt I called my son. But the more they were called, the more they went away from me.*
v. 1,2

'When Israel was a child, I loved him . . .'

The man had one son. And then came the news that another son had been born to him. His heart overflowed with happiness. He loved those boys. He watched out for them, taught them new things, gave them a good life. They were his pride and joy.
As they grew up, the boys realized that they enjoyed luxuries other children didn't. Their father must be rich.
'Daddy, why are you rich?'

'. . . and out of Egypt I called my son.'

The man hadn't always been rich. He knew what it was like to struggle, to be hungry, to have nowhere to sleep. He was rich because he never wanted his children to experience those things. Long before either of his sons was born, the man determined to do everything in his power to provide for his future children. It meant he was mocked by people who didn't understand, who thought he was crazy, or too big for his boots. But the man carried on regardless. He worked and worked and saved and saved. He went without, so his children would never need to.

And they didn't need to. As they grew, the boys learned the family business. 'One day,' said their father, 'one day, this will all be yours.' The boys looked round the estate with amazement. Such a big and beautiful thing would actually be theirs one day?

'But the more they were called, the more they went away from me.'

The boys grew into young men. Now they worked alongside their father. Once, watching his younger son at work in the barn, the man noticed something he couldn't quite figure out. His son seemed restless. Going over to the barn, he put his hand on the young man's shoulder. 'You're doing a great job, son.' The next day, the man saw his son out in the fields. Hopefully the encouragement yesterday had done the trick. Drawing closer, he saw the downcast slump of his son's shoulders as the young man gazed into the distance before resuming his work. 'Well done, son.' Day after day, the man encouraged his son. He called to him, whenever he could: 'That's really good, son.' But the restlessness increased. The shoulders slumped more. The eyes gazed frequently into the distance.

And then, one day, his son was gone. 'Bye, Dad.' The son turned his back and resolutely walked away from his father. The man called after him, louder and louder, 'Come back! Please come back. Please . . .' But the son didn't even turn around.[1]

When you were a child, God loved you.

> *See what great love the Father has lavished on us, that*
> *we should be called children of God!*
> *And that is what we are!*
>
> 1 John 3:1

You're still a child.
You're not expected to have it all sorted.
And that's OK.
More than OK.
Father God delights in you.
He loves you.
Lavishly.

And, out of the shadows, he called you.

> *You are a chosen people . . . [God] called you out of dark-*
> *ness into his wonderful light.*
>
> 1 Peter 2:9

Out of darkness, God called you. 'Come to me.'
Out of ongoing darkness, out of every darkness you face.
'Come to me.'
Jesus said, 'I am the light of the world.'[2]
Even the dark bits in your world.
'Come to me.'
The light didn't just happen.
Jesus left the light of heaven – brighter than any other light –
and came down into the darkness of the world. So dark, no
light could ever reach it. Unless Jesus said:
**I'll go to the cross. I'll die. I'll face the darkest dark, so
God's children never need to.**
Hanging there, Jesus cried, 'It is finished.'[3]
Darkness is dealt with.

> *Praise be to the God and Father of our Lord Jesus Christ!
> In his great mercy he has given us new birth into a liv-
> ing hope through the resurrection of Jesus Christ from
> the dead, and into an inheritance that can never perish,
> spoil or fade. This inheritance is kept in heaven for you.*
>                                        1 Peter 1:3,4

'But the more they were called, the more they went away
from me.'

**I love you**, says God. I'm what you need, says the world.
**Come to me**, says God. No, come to *me*, tempts the
world.
**We can work together**, says God. No, you're better alone,
insists the world.

**It's you I want**, says God. No, why would he want *you*? sneers the world.

The son didn't turn around, but neither did the father. Day after day, he watched over the way his son had gone. He watched and waited and longed for his son to return.

Eventually, his son returned. Before, the son, dressed in all the arrogance of self-reliance, had refused to turn around and look at his father.

Now, dressed in the rags of shattered dreams, his father was the only way he could look.

As he looked, his eyes met his dad's.

'I never stopped looking for you, son.'

> *I have loved you with an everlasting love; I have drawn you with unfailing kindness.*
> *I will build you up again, and you, Virgin Israel, will be rebuilt.*
>
> Jeremiah 31:3,4

Israel knew what it was to be loved by God. They had experienced him with them in an amazing way as he led them through the desert. He'd fed them when there was no food, provided water when there was none, helped them to victory over enemies, healed them from illness.

Mountain top moments.

Israel also knew what it was to feel far from God. To feel let down by him. To complain about him. To wish they'd died.

Valley moments.

And God says, 'I will build you up again.'
**You don't have to do it on your own.**
But sometimes we doubt. The valleys are so present. The 'I will build you up' promise echoes hollow in our empty selves.

There is always hope in our hopelessness. A voice in that echo:

'And you . . . will be rebuilt.'

It's not an empty promise. God's promises never are.

> *For no matter how many promises God has made, they are 'Yes' in Christ.*
>
> 2 Corinthians 1:20

And he's the only one who can promise them.

Sometimes, my nephew asks me to help him build something with his building blocks. So we kneel together on the floor and begin to build. As we do, he instructs me 'make the wall higher, don't put that brick there, build a pathway' etc.

He has the vision in his head and, unless I allow him to be in charge, unless I follow his instructions, his vision won't happen.

I have no problem following his instructions. I'm happy to. I want to. Because I want to see what he has in mind.

Sometimes I get it wrong, though. My ideas take over. I forget how much I want to see his design. And I build the wall a little higher. It looks out of place and I take it down.

It doesn't work. Caleb leans over and rebuilds it so that it fits. I should have remembered who was the boss.

'I will build you up again, and you . . . will be rebuilt.'

So often, I rewrite this verse: 'I will build me up again . . .'

It's OK God. I know what needs to be done. I have the plans. You can be my assistant.

I try and try.

It doesn't work.

And I sit in the rubble of my life, clutching my plans.

God leans over and loosens my grip. I let go of my plans. He takes them and rips them up.

**I will build you up again, and you, Emily, will be rebuilt.**

God will build me up again: he promised.

I will be rebuilt: God promised.

From the rubble, look up. Your eyes will meet his.

He loves you with an everlasting love. He draws you with loving kindness.

He builds you up. And you will be rebuilt. You will.

*And we all, who with unveiled faces contemplate the Lord's glory, are being transformed into his image with ever-increasing glory, which comes from the Lord, who is the Spirit.*

2 Corinthians 3:18

*I'm rubble for rebuilding.*
**You're rubble for rebuilding?**
**Perfect. That's where I come in.**
*I'm rubble being rebuilt.*
**You're rubble being rebuilt?**

**You certainly are. I should know.**
*I'm . . .*
**You're rubble rebuilt.**
*I'm rubble again.*
**I know what you are.**
**I know where you are.**
**I know who you are.**
**I build you up.**
**Again and again.**
**And, every time,**
**however many times there are,**
**you will be rebuilt.**

*The LORD upholds all who fall and lifts up all who are bowed down.*

Psalm 145:14


Father God
Thank you that I can be rebuilt.
I can always be rebuilt.
By you.
Help me not to try to take over.
Amen

## REFLECTION

- Are you restless?
- Where do you need to be rebuilt?
- Is God your assistant, or are you his?
- God watches for you. Do you watch for him?
- At the end of each day, thank God for watching all you've lived that day.

## GOD'S CALLING CARD

# 9

# **Ananias**
(Acts 9)

 *In Damascus there was a disciple named Ananias. The Lord called to him in a vision, 'Ananias!'*

v. 10

The nudge from God happened at the end of a session at a large Christian conference. I was, by choice, sitting on my own, reflecting on the evening's session. Others around me did the same, as the band played gentle music (I saw fingers on keyboards, which is how I know it was gentle). Then the nudge: **Emily, see that person over there? Go and talk to them.** I didn't want to. I wanted to stay where I was. So I didn't go. The nudge came again: **Emily, see that person over there? Go and talk to them.** 'No.' **Emily** . . . Eventually, after more nudges than I care to admit, I went. I sat down beside them, and we talked. Then we prayed. 'We' being someone who it turned out was terrified because they were losing their hearing, and me, someone – perhaps the only someone at the conference – who knew that fear. **Emily, see that person over there? Go and talk to them.** God knew best.

Everyone is talking about this man named Saul. Us Followers of the Way (Christians) are petrified of him. He hates us and wants to throw us in prison. All because we follow Jesus. I've decided to steer well clear of him.

Father God
Help me to be open to relationship with others.
Amen

I recognized the voice straight away, calling my name.

Close enough to call.

   *'Ananias!'*
   *'Yes, Lord'.*

Ananias had spent time with God, learning to recognize God's voice.
I sometimes meet people who are blind. I am always amazed by the fact that when I've spoken with them once, they subsequently know who I am when they hear my voice. They recognize people by their voices.
They know who I am and, therefore, they know who I'm not. They don't confuse my voice with someone else's.
Get to know God's voice.
Don't confuse it with other voices.

> *Whether you turn to the right or to the left, your ears will hear a voice behind you, saying,*
> *'This is the way; walk in it.'*

Isaiah 30:21

God speaks.

What's he saying to you? Right now?

Maybe you don't think he's saying anything.

Lying on a bed, I reached some double doors. No access. That is, no access unless you're involved in surgery. I was involved in surgery. I'd be going through those doors hearing, and coming back out hearing nothing. The surgery, in saving my life, would take my hearing.

My parents weren't involved in the surgery. They couldn't go through those doors. The words they said to me now were to be the last words I'd hear them say. Ever.

'I love you.'

The last words I heard them say.

'I love you.'

'I love you' can always be the last words you heard God say. Because he says them all the time. Through everything that happens in life, runs a constant from God: I love you. Walk in his love.

A man runs. By running, he is breaking with protocol. Men didn't run. But the man is running to Jesus. And Jesus is more important to him than the demands of society. His story is related in Mark 10:17–31.

Falling on his knees in front of Jesus, the man asks, 'What can I do to inherit eternal life?'

Jesus lists the commandments: Do not murder, or steal, or cheat . . .

The man is relieved. 'I've kept those commandments all my life.'

And, as he kneels in the dust, hot and dishevelled from running, full of self-sufficiency and boasting, Jesus looks at him.

'Jesus looked at him and loved him' (v. 21).

The man was a mess, inside as well as out. Jesus knew. And Jesus looked at him – at the mess – and loved him.

Let God look at you.

Maybe you are messy.

But you are loved.

> Father God
> Thank you for seeing me.
> Thank you for knowing me.
> Thank you for loving me.
> Amen

Jesus loved him even though he knew what was about to take place:

'There's something more you need to do. Give all your money to the poor. Then your treasure will truly be in heaven.'

How tightly do we cling to material wealth?

When he heard Jesus' words, the man went away sad.

He was very rich.

He couldn't give that up.

And so he went away sad.

In turning his back on Jesus and walking away, he was allowing what he couldn't do to obliterate the love Jesus had for him.

He turned his back on love that said, **I see you and I love you.**

Don't allow what you can't do to obliterate love.
God sees you and he loves you.

> *For I am convinced that neither death nor life, neither angels nor demons, neither the present nor the future, nor any powers, neither height nor depth, nor anything else in all creation, will be able to separate us from the love of God that is in Christ Jesus our Lord.*
>
> Romans 8:38,39

*'Ananias!'*
*'Yes, Lord.'*

Ananias knew immediately who was speaking to him.
He recognized God's voice.
And he called him Lord.
A Lord is one who rules, or a master.
By saying 'Lord', Ananias was already in a place which said, 'I'm not in charge.'
Hudson Taylor, a man who went as a missionary to China, said, 'Christ is either Lord of all, or is not Lord at all.'[1]
Could you call God Lord?

Father God
Help me to call you Lord
and mean it.
Amen

Basically, God told me to go to a particular house and ask for Saul! The Saul I've been avoiding. The Saul who is persecuting Christians like me. 'Go and ask for Saul. He's had a vision, and he saw a man called Ananias – you – put his hands on him and restore his sight.'

Saul had lost his sight. In doing so, he recognized Jesus. Previously, he'd wanted nothing to do with Jesus, other than to ridicule him and his followers. And God, on the Damascus road (see Acts 9), broke in.[2] A flash of light, which said, 'Stop looking, just listen.'

Sometimes, we need to stop looking.

For Saul, looking meant relying on his own strength. What he could do. His impressive academic qualifications, his ability to exploit people, his certainty that he was right, his prestige. And God said, **Stop looking.**

In Philippians 3, Paul (who changed his name from Saul), gives a mini CV. It's impressive. Paul says, I have every reason to put my confidence in myself. I was born into the right family, trained under the best tutors, followed the law to the letter. But . . .

> *Whatever were gains to me I now consider loss for the sake of Christ. What is more, I consider everything a loss because of the surpassing worth of knowing Christ Jesus my Lord.*

> vv. 7,8

In other words, nothing was more important than Jesus. Not status, or qualifications, or prestige . . .

And, unlike the rich young ruler, Paul didn't go away from Jesus sad.

*I want to know Christ.*
v. 10

**Stop looking.**
Knowing Jesus was of 'surpassing worth'.
Worth more than all else put together.
Knowing Jesus is better than everything.
We don't need to keep looking for anything better,
because there isn't anything.
But so often we do look.
**Stop looking.**
We take our eyes off the One we should never stop seeing,
and we start looking at other options.
Just in case.
**Stop looking.**
Knowing Jesus is worth more than being known by the world.

Father God
Help me to stop looking at anything but you.
I want to know you more and more.
Amen

Saul met Jesus when he stopped looking.
Often, when people pray, they close their eyes. They don't have to, but it does help shut out other distractions. Things that jostle for their attention as they talk to God.

*We live by faith, not by sight.*
       2 Corinthians 5:7

We need to learn to stop looking.

If we do live by faith, we can't live by sight. The two are incompatible. And yet how often we try to force them to work together.

I often think I'm happy to do what God wants, so long as he tells me what that is. I want to know what's ahead. In a way, I want to see the future. I want faith with sight.

I need to learn to stop looking.

Faith, not sight.

> *'I know the plans I have for you,' declares the LORD, 'plans to prosper you and not to harm you, plans to give you hope and a future.'*
>
>                              Jeremiah 29:10,11

**I care about you enough to prepare a plan for you.**
**I know . . .**

Is that enough?

Absolute trust.

Faith not sight.

Can we trust the One who knows our future? He is trustworthy, so how can we be trusting?

I had a conversation with someone who was concerned about the future. Things were up in the air, certain events might or might not happen, it was worrying. Add to that the worry that she couldn't seem to trust it to God. She wanted to, but couldn't. It was too big.

As we chatted, we realized the importance of 'today'. Trust God today. Now. And, one day, that future she'd been worrying about – the future he knew – would be today.
And she'd be trusting God in it.
Trust God today.
Today I trust God.

> *[Jesus said] 'Do not worry about tomorrow.'*
>
> Matthew 6:34

When I was at junior school, we'd sing a song in assembly: 'He's Got the Whole World in His Hands'.[3]
Remember, the whole world includes you.
God's got your world in his hands.
And he wants you to know that.

> *[He says] 'See, I have engraved you on the palms of my hands.'*
>
> Isaiah 49:16

Do you see what he wants you to see?
Engraved. Permanent.
Your world in his hands.
Today I trust God.

Father God
Today I trust you.
Help me trust you today.
Amen

I said, 'Hang on a minute. This is the man who is trying to arrest Christians!' He was the last person I wanted to see.

Ananias is told 'go to Saul'. It was such a shock, and he was thrown into panic. So, in that moment, he missed part of God's plan.

An amazing part.

God was going to restore someone's sight!

And Ananias was so busy focusing on the 'go to Saul' part, that he forgot to focus on what God was doing.

God is all around. Let's not miss what he's doing.

God said 'Go!'

Go. Stop thinking. And obey.

In Matthew 14, Peter is faced with a choice. He's in a boat, on a stormy sea, and he sees Jesus walking towards him on the water. Can he be imagining things? 'Lord, if it's really you, tell me to walk on the water towards you.' 'Come,' says Jesus.

So Peter has established that it's really Jesus, Jesus has told him to get out of the boat and walk on water, and he does. There he is, knowing 100 per cent that Jesus is with him, walking on water (!), and he begins to doubt. Amid absolute certainty in God, he doubts. He looks around. He sees all that could go wrong. Which is when things do start to go wrong. Peter begins to drown, and Jesus reaches down and saves him.

Ananias knew God. He knew his voice. He knew it wasn't just anyone telling him to go to Saul. And yet, amid absolute certainty that he's hearing from God, he looks at the facts from a human viewpoint.

*As the heavens are higher than the earth, so are my ways higher than your ways and my thoughts than your thoughts.*

Isaiah 55:9

Sometimes, the best thing we can do is simply remind ourselves that God is God, and we are not.
**I am God.**
**You know that.**
**So be still.**

*But the Lord said to Ananias, 'Go! This man is my chosen instrument to proclaim my name to the Gentiles and their kings and to the people of Israel. I will show him how much he must suffer for my name.*

Acts 9:15,16

*Before I formed you in the womb I knew you.*

Jeremiah 1:5

Some Bible versions translate the word 'knew' as 'chose'.
Before you were created, before you did a single thing, God chose you.
Just because you're you.
**I chose you.**
'I've chosen this man.'
'He will suffer.'
God doesn't say, 'Oops, I've chosen him, but things will be difficult, so I'd better un-choose him.'
No. **I've chosen him.** A declaration that nothing can change.

God's chosen you.
And nothing can change that.


> Father God
> You chose me.
> Amen


Saul (later, Paul) will suffer. He will go through hard times. We can look at this in two ways.

One is to ask how God could be so cruel. How could a loving, all-powerful God possibly know that hard things are coming in our lives and yet not do anything to stop them? Why? Why?

And the voice breaks in:

**I am God.**

**You know that.**

**So be still.**

In letting go of our need to understand the incomprehensible, of trying to be more than we are, of trying to take the place of God, we are free to find release even in our pain.

Jesus, on the cross, suffered. He was thirsty, he was ridiculed, he saw his family suffering, he was exposed to physical torture, and what did he say?

> *Father, into your hands I commit my spirit.*
>
> Luke 23:46


I let go. I choose to have you in charge of me. I don't have to fight my circumstances. I can be still, even in the midst of them.

'Father, into your hands I commit my spirit.'
That's the other way we can look at it.

Father God
Thank you that my whys, and my world,
are in your hands.
Amen

Jesus is quoting Psalm 31:5 here. It's a good example to follow.

Repetition.

Do you have words that you repeat to yourself? Words you can say when you don't know what to say?
I do. I particularly repeat them in hard times. One of those times is during my annual MRI scan, which I have to assess the progress – or lack of, maybe – of my tumours. Encased in the scanning machine, which is like a tunnel, unable to see beyond the roof of the tunnel, which is inches from my nose, and of course unable to hear anything, I whisper to myself, again and again: 'It is well with my soul.'
Words penned by someone who lost most of his business in the great Chicago fire of 1871. Someone who lost all four of his children when their ship sank at sea.
And yet Spafford could write, 'It is well with my soul.'
Not only write it, but write it as he later journeyed across the Atlantic, the place where his children drowned.
'It is well with my soul.'

Not written in a pretence everything was fine, but despite the fact everything was not fine.

Often, my 'it is well with my soul' is said through tears, through pain, through bewilderment. Yet, as I say it, repeating it over and over, I realize again the truth of it. 'Though trials should come . . . it is well with my soul.'[4]

God chose me.
Into your hands I commit my spirit.
It is well with my soul.

In John 16, Jesus tells his disciples about the difficulties they will face. The hardships, the persecution, the rejection. And he tells them why he's done so:

> *I have told you these things, so that in me you may have peace. In this world you will have trouble. But take heart! I have overcome the world.*

> John 16:33

When faced with hard times, peace is possible. Inner peace. 'It is well with my soul' peace.

**I am God.**
**You know that.**
**So be still.**

In John 15, again talking about suffering, Jesus reminds his disciples, more than once, that he has chosen them.

Father God
You chose me.
Into your hands I commit my life.
It is well with my soul.
Amen

*Then Ananias went to the house and entered it. Placing his hands on Saul, he said, 'Brother Saul, the Lord — Jesus, who appeared to you on the road as you were coming here — has sent me so that you may see again and be filled with the Holy Spirit.' Immediately, something like scales fell from Saul's eyes, and he could see again. He got up and was baptised, and after taking some food, he regained his strength.*

Acts 9:17–19

Ananias went, in obedience to God's instructions, and he called Saul 'brother'. This man, who he'd tried to persuade God he didn't want to be anywhere near, he calls 'brother'.

Brother means family. Related. Sharing. Not necessarily being the best of friends all the time but, despite differences, there is an underlying similarity. Shared genes. Shared DNA. Shared family.

Ananias now focused on the similarities.

Brother Saul.

Sometimes, as Christians, we can be good at focusing on the differences.

You set out your chairs in rows? We always have a circle.

You have PowerPoint? We always have hymn-books.

You have a worship band? We have one piano.

You start your service at 10 a.m.? We start at 10.30.

Let's not forget to be like Ananias:

You have Jesus? We have Jesus.


It did take Ananias time to be able to focus on the similarities between himself and Saul. Ananias was terrified of him. Most probably, some of Ananias' friends had been arrested by him. Ananias had been hurt by him.

How did Ananias reach a place where he could go to Saul? Where he could step over their differences to: 'You have Jesus? I have Jesus.'

Through the grace of God.

'My grace is sufficient for you . . . '[5]

How can we be like Ananias?

Through the grace of God.

'My grace is sufficient for you . . . '

You have Jesus? I have Jesus.

'Brother Saul . . . '


Father God

Thank you for your all sufficient grace.

Amen

Realistically, we will have differences. And sometimes, despite the things we share, those differences loom large. As Ananias experienced, people hurt us. And that's hard.

I remember one such time. I was angry, I was hurting. I didn't like it much. I ranted to God about the unfairness of it all.

He asked, **Have you prayed for the person?**

I ranted on. Of course I had. I was praying about them right now, wasn't I?

**Have you prayed for the person?**

Well, yes. I was praying that they'd change their ways right now, wasn't I?

**Have you prayed for the person?**

I stopped. Prayer is a blessing from God. Praying for someone means blessing them. Could I do that? Could I ask God to bless the person who was hurting me?

I tried it, through gritted teeth. 'God bless them, Amen.' I was still angry at them.

But the next day, I prayed it again. 'God bless them, Amen.' I was still angry. But my teeth were slightly less clenched.

Day after day, I prayed, 'God bless them, Amen.'

My teeth weren't clenched any more. I was no longer angry. It's hard to stay angry at someone you're asking God to bless.

*The LORD bless you and keep you; the LORD make his face shine on you and be gracious to you; the LORD turn his face towards you and give you peace.* (Amen.)

Numbers 6:24–26

Ananias told Saul that Jesus has 'sent me so that you may see again'.

Saul had once been able to see. Now he couldn't, and he needed someone to help. Someone willing to allow God to work through them in order to restore Saul's sight.

*You are the light of the world. A town built on a hill cannot be hidden. Neither do people light a lamp and put it under a bowl. Instead they put it on its stand, and it gives light to everyone in the house. In the same way, let your light shine before others, that they may see your good deeds and glorify your Father in heaven.*

Matthew 5:14–16

Remember, Jesus said, 'I am the light of the world.'[6]
As we allow him to work through us, it's his light that shines.
His light that allows people to see.
Him who is glorified.
Let your light shine.

God called into Ananias' normality. Into his everyday living in tune with the voice of God. And God clothed him in friendship.
**I want you to go to Saul and restore his sight, because I have a job for him to do.**
Because I have a job for him to do.
God told Ananias why. He let Ananias into his thinking. As friends do.

*You are my friends if you do what I command. I no longer call you servants, because a servant does not know his master's business. Instead, I have called you friends, for everything that I learned from my Father I have made known to you.*

John 15:14,15

Clothed in friendship with God.

> *There is a friend who sticks closer than a brother.*
>
> Proverbs 18:24

*My soul?*
*Listen to me.*
*It is well.*
*I know you're pulled in all directions*
*and it's hard*
*and you're tired.*
*Trust God today.*
*And know, my soul;*
*it is well.*
*I know you're overwhelmed*
*and your diary is exploding*
*and your head is bursting.*
*Trust God today.*
*And know, my soul;*
*it is well.*
*I know you're in pain.*
*Poorly.*
*Hurting.*
*Helpless.*
*Trust God today.*
*And know, my soul;*
*it is well.*
*I know you're scared.*
*Future looms bleak*
*with tomorrows of fear.*

*Trust God today.*
*And know, my soul;*
*it is well.*
*Every today,*
*trust God*
*and know.*
*Listen to me,*
*my soul:*
*It is well.*

*From the ends of the earth I call to you, I call as my heart*
*grows faint; lead me to the rock that is higher than I.*

Psalm 61:2

Father God
I do look.
A lot.
I look at the things I don't have
but I want.
I look at the person I think I should be
but am not.
Help me to remember that you look, too.
You look at me,
in all my looking,
and you love me.
May your looking cause me to
stop looking.
Amen

## REFLECTION

- How do you treat Jesus-followers?
- Do you make people want to steer clear of you?
- What names do you give God?
- Do you believe God looks at you with love?
- Where do you need to stop looking?
- Do you focus on differences with people, or on similarities?
- Who can you ask Jesus to bless this week?
- Whisper it is well with my soul.

## GOD'S CALLING CARD

# 10

# God
(Jeremiah 33)

 *Call to me and I will answer you and tell you great and unsearchable things you do not know.*

v. 3

Being in hospital, newly deafened, was a scary experience. And then I developed an eye infection which meant that every night both my eyes needed to be taped shut. I'd spend the next hours in pitch black and silent terror.

One evening, a nurse approached me, carrying the roll of tape. I steeled myself, lay back on the pillows and closed my eyes. I knew the drill by now. Except the tape did not come. I opened my eyes and saw the nurse, tape in hand, standing by my bed just looking at me. Then she picked up the pad of paper I used to communicate, and wrote some words on it: 'It must be scary?'

I swallowed hard, and nodded.

She wrote some more on the paper, then gave it to me to read.

'If you need anything in the night, press the call button I'm about to put in your hand. If you press it, I will come . . .'

I will come. Not anyone else. Me.

'. . . and, when I do, I will take your hand, and touch your fingers to my ring. So you know for sure that it's me. You know who is helping you.'

'Call to me and I will answer you and tell you great and unsearchable things you do not know.'
**Call to me, Jeremiah.**
**Bring me into your situation.**

In an amazing paradox of vulnerability, God asks us to call with a purpose, as he calls with a purpose.

Jeremiah has been prophesying from God that Jerusalem will be destroyed. King Zedekiah doesn't like that one bit so, after repeated and unsuccessful attempts to persuade Jeremiah to change his prophecy, he places Jeremiah under house arrest.

Jeremiah is trapped, his freedom taken away, in a sort of prison; things aren't looking great, and into that, God said, 'Call to me . . .'

In the same way – using the same root word – as God had called Abraham, Moses and the rest, God said, 'Call to me . . .'

Remember Hagar? Running into the desert, collapsing in despair, waiting to die, and God asked, 'What's the matter?'

God cares enough to find us in the wasteland. To be with us in our desert places. To ask us what's the matter.

Wherever you are, he'll find you.

> *If I go up to the heavens, you are there; if I make my bed in the depths, you are there.*
> *If I rise on the wings of the dawn, if I settle on the far side of the sea, even there your hand will guide me, your right hand will hold me fast.*
>
> Psalm 139:8–10

Father God
Thank you for always finding me.
Amen

Yet God, in his grace, offers more.
'Call to me . . .'

'Call to me and I will answer you and tell you great and unsearchable things you do not know.'

We don't have to wait. We can call upon God at any time. From anywhere. Even from prison, from restrictions, from frustration, from lack of freedom, from a place of being bullied, we can always call.

We've been calling to God throughout this book. Short calls, longer calls, shared calls, calls only you know. Calls between you and God and no one else.
The prayers have been calling.
Have you called?

Pause to call throughout life, too.
Ask for God's presence.

'Call to me . . .'
**Invite me to come into your situation.**
**Press your buzzer.**
**And know I will always come.**
The nurse didn't need to know what was wrong before
she came. I didn't need to explain it to her, so she could
make an informed decision about whether to come. She
just came.
Press your buzzer. Call to God. You don't need to explain
why. He knows anyway. Don't struggle for words. Just let
him come.
He will always come.

*God is our refuge and strength, an ever-present help . . .*
Psalm 46:1

Father God
Help me to keep calling.
Amen

'Call to me . . .'
God has been speaking to Jeremiah a lot, and Jeremiah has
been speaking to him. They've had many conversations.
God knows Jeremiah is in a good relationship with him.
Suddenly, in the midst of it all, he says:
**Jeremiah? Call to me.**
**Take the initiative.**

**Call to me because you choose to.**
God doesn't only invite us to call to him;
he wants us to call to him.
'Call to me and I will answer you . . .'
He likes it when we call.
**You can call to me. Please will you?**
**I'm here.**
'I call with all my heart'[1] . . . but I don't always know what
to say.
**I will answer the wordless longings of your heart.**
**I will answer them with myself.**
**Just call to me.**
**Please?**
Moses asked God, who are you?
And God replied, 'I AM WHO I AM.'[2]
And that was enough.
**I am God.**
**You know that.**
**So be still.**
**I AM WHO I AM.**
**It's enough.**
**Please will you choose to call?**

Father God
Thank you for wanting my call.
Amen

'Call to me and I will answer you and tell you great and
unsearchable things you do not know.'

So we call. God answers. And he tells us things we don't know.

> *'What no eye has seen, what no ear has heard and what no human mind has conceived' – the things God has prepared for those who love him.*
>
> 1 Corinthians 2:9

Prepared by God, just for you. Even better than you can possibly imagine.

More than enough.

> *Your path led through the sea, your way through the mighty waters, though your footprints were not seen. You led your people like a flock.*
>
> Psalm 77:19,20

I'm not a shepherd. Apart from a family holiday on a farm as a child, during which I was allowed to watch the shepherd caring for his sheep, I have had very little contact with sheep beyond noticing white 'clouds' in fields as I pass by. The holiday happened at sheep dipping time. Each sheep in the flock was plunged into a trough of smelly liquid, in order to protect the sheep from infestation. It didn't look very pleasant for the sheep, I have to say. Afterwards, the dripping wet huddle of sheep just stood in a rather sorry-looking group. They didn't know what to do.

And then the shepherd came. He called them to follow. They recognized his voice. So they followed him.

Apparently, if someone else had called, they wouldn't have gone. They recognized the call of their shepherd.

The shepherd explained to me that he needed to stay in front of the sheep. They needed to follow, not lead. Because they didn't know how to lead.

So the shepherd went first, calling to them along the way, to reassure them.

To show them the way.

To encourage them to keep going.

The path they were treading was safe, because their shepherd has been there first.

In a way, the shepherd leaves calling cards. 'I've been here' reminders. To reassure the sheep that the way they are going is safe, because their shepherd has been there first.

Jesus is our Shepherd.

> *I am the good shepherd; I know my sheep and my sheep know me.*
>
> John 10:14

We've looked at some of the calling cards our Shepherd leaves. Reminding us that we belong, that we can hold on to God, that God's grace provides for all we need. Reminding us that we can believe, to remember God, to grow closer to him, to glorify him in our lives. Reminding us that God rebuilds us, again and again, that we can trust him, and call to him.

In the nineteenth century, visitors to a house would give their calling card to the butler, who would establish whether the home-owner was available.[3] If it was a first visit, the visitor would immediately leave after presenting the card, whether or not the owner was at home. It was then down to the recipient to choose if they would like to start a friendship. If they did, they returned a calling card. They called back.

Keep looking for God's calling cards. Things which remind you he's there.

And choose to call back.

Father God
I'm calling back.
Amen

*When he [the shepherd] has brought out all his own, he goes on ahead of them, and his sheep follow him because they know his voice. But they will never follow a stranger; in fact, they will run away from him because they do not recognise a stranger's voice.*

vv. 4,5

How did the sheep know the Shepherd's voice? They'd heard it before.

Just as Ananias recognized God's voice.

What did the sheep do when they heard a voice not their shepherd's? They ran away from it.

'. . . they will never follow a stranger . . .'

Do you? Do you follow the voices around you? Voices you don't recognize?

Learn to know your Shepherd's voice.

I was shopping with a friend and her two daughters, aged 9 and 7. I know them well, I've watched the girls grow up. So, when the girls chose something small they'd like to buy, I knew it was safe to give them some money and let them make the purchase themselves. They'd never been in the shop before but they know me, they know their mum, and we were there. They went to the counter, bought their gifts, and came back to us.

They came back, as I knew they would. The transaction went well, too. I know because I stood at a distance, watching. Checking the girls were safe.

I also know they would 'never follow a stranger'.

'Follow' in this verse means to accompany, travel with, or partner.

Could God say of you: **He/she will never accompany a stranger; never deliberately spend time with a voice they don't recognize as mine.**

'in fact, they will run away from [a stranger] . . .'

In other words, the sheep turn their back on a voice they don't recognize as their shepherd's.

Sometimes, we need to do the same.

When voices press in, it can be hard to know what is God, what is us, what is other people, what is the world. A cacophony of confusion.

Don't recognize a voice?

Turn your back. Stop focusing on that voice for a bit, and call out to God.

Father God

Is this your voice?

Amen

The God who will answer.

Yet, sometimes, we can convince ourselves that it must be God, because everything seems to be working out.

Take, for example, Jonah.

God said, **'Jonah, go to Nineveh, and tell the people there to repent.'**

Jonah didn't want to do that. So he ran in the opposite direction. He wanted to go to Tarshish, but he'd need to go by boat. When he arrived at the port, there was a ship about to leave . . . for Tarshish.

**Jonah, go to Nineveh, and tell the people there to repent.**

Well, I think that's what God said. OK, I know he did, but look. There's a boat which will take me away from Nineveh. God could have stopped that couldn't he, but he didn't.

**Jonah, go to Nineveh, and tell the people there to repent.**

And look; I've just checked my money and I've got enough to pay my fare. God could have stopped that, couldn't he, but he didn't.

**Jonah, go to Nineveh, and tell the people there to repent.**

There's space for me on the boat, even though I didn't book in advance. God could have stopped that, couldn't he, but he didn't.

**Jonah, go to Nineveh, and tell the people there to repent.**

The ship set sail. There was an almighty storm. Jonah ended up being thrown overboard and swallowed by a big fish, which eventually spat him out onto a beach.

**Jonah, go to Nineveh, and tell the people there to repent.**

And, finally, Jonah went to Nineveh.
But what did Jonah do inside that fish?

> *In my distress I called to the LORD, and he answered me.*
>
> Jonah 2:2

'Call to me and I will answer you and tell you great and unsearchable things you do not know.'

> *Then the word of the LORD came to Jonah a second time: 'Go to the great city of Nineveh and proclaim to it the message I give you.'*
>
> Jonah 3:1,2

Jonah called out to God, and God repeated what he'd said before.

God doesn't change. It was Jonah who repeatedly refused to accept what God was saying. Go to Nineveh? No, not me.

It wasn't nice, refusing to accept what God was saying. It led to a lot of worry, and turmoil. But Jonah kept going until, at the lowest of the low, stuck in the belly of a fish for three days, he called out to God. In his distress, God was still there. Jonah called. And God answered.

Father God
Thank you for not ignoring me.
Amen

And God told him again.
**Jonah, go to Ninevah . . .**
God simply repeated what Jonah had already been told. And yet Jonah hadn't really taken those words to heart. He didn't know them. They were 'great and unsearchable things you do not know'.
And God told him again.

We have a patient God. He tells us things over and over again.
**My child, I love you.**
*I don't believe that. I'm unlovable. Someone told me so the other day. You could have stopped them saying that, but you didn't.*
**My child, I love you.**
*I don't believe that. I'm unlovable. I'm not very pretty, or intelligent, or fun to be around. You could have made me differently, but you didn't.*
**My child, I love you.**

*I don't believe that. I'm unlovable. You could have made me differently, but you didn't.*

**My child, I love you.**

*I don't believe that. I'm unlovable. I've looked everywhere for love, but it's nowhere. Apart from being something other people have. You could have made me differently, but you didn't.*

**My child, I love you.**

*I don't believe that. You could have made me differently, but you didn't.*

**I know.**

**Because I love you.**

**When I say 'I love you'**

**I mean 'you're precious in my sight'.**[4]

**I made you.**

**I could have made anything I wanted.**

**So I did.**

**'Call to me and I will answer you and tell you great and unsearchable things you do not know': My child, I love you.**

Know that you are loved.
And don't ever convince yourself otherwise.

> *May the Lord direct your hearts into God's love.*
> 2 Thessalonians 3:5

*Voices surround me,*
*blurring to noise as*
*they compete for my attention.*

*Telling me*
*what I should be,*
*what I shouldn't be,*
*what I need,*
*what I don't need.*
*I don't know how they know,*
*but they seem so sure.*
*So confident.*
*They scare me.*
*Like wolves, they circle me,*
*licking their lips,*
*telling me if I follow them*
*my fear will go.*
*I will be what I should be,*
*I will have what I need.*
*My feet won't move.*
*I'm too scared.*
*The voices surrounding me*
*fade to nothing*
*at my Shepherd's call.*
*I'm safe.*

> *My sheep listen to my voice; I know them, and they fol-*
> *low me. I give them eternal life, and they shall never*
> *perish; no one will snatch them out of my hand.*
>
> John 10:27,28

Father God
Thank you that I can always call to you.
You always listen.
You always come.
I'm often like Jonah,
going my own way.
I forget to call
until I'm desperate.
Lost.
Alone.
Yet my call, when it comes,
reaches you.
And you answer.
Every time.
Thank you for loving me so much.
Amen

## REFLECTION

- Do you think God wants to help you?
- What do you learn about God from the fact that he wants you to take the initiative and choose to call him?
- Do you think not knowing everything is a good thing?
- On a scale of one to ten, how good are you at being a sheep?
- Call to God.

## GOD'S CALLING CARD

# 11

# Paul

(Philippians 3)

 *I press on towards the goal to win the prize for which God has called me heavenwards in Christ Jesus.*

v. 14

Little faces look out of the window, noses pressed to the glass, eyes moving up and down the road. This happens every time I visit my nieces and nephews. They're excited to see me, and look out for me, because they don't want to miss a minute.

Last time I went to visit one of my sisters and her family, I was staying for a couple of nights. I'd hardly got through the front door before 6-year-old Abigail welcomed me. Grabbing my hand, she dragged me up the stairs. 'You're sleeping in my bedroom!' she announced. 'I'll show you.' She showed me her little desk where 'we will sit and make jewellery tomorrow'. She showed me her bookshelf – 'You can read that book to me at bedtime'. She showed me her owl-adorned curtains – 'Make sure you close them all the way so the light doesn't get in.' She showed me how to reach a hard-to-get-to switch, so I could turn on her pretty butterfly lights. She showed me a vase of flowers – 'I chose these ones for you because they are purple.' She showed me a card stuck on her wall – 'Remember you sent me this card?' She showed me stripy rabbit sitting on my bed. Stripy rabbit is her favourite toy, which she takes to bed every night, but 'you can have him in your bed while you are here'.

'I press on towards the goal to win the prize for which God has called me heavenwards in Christ Jesus.'

Called here means 'vocation'. As some would say, for example, 'being a nurse is my calling'.

The 'prize' is living with Christ Jesus.

Paul is saying his life's calling is to keep heaven in mind. It's a vocation given to him by God.

In pressing on to take hold of the prize, Paul is moving heavenwards. He's not there yet, but he's heading in the right direction.

He's travelling the heavenwards road.

It's a calling given to all of us. To you. To me. Keep 'heavenwards' in mind as we travel.

This is the kingdom of God.

> *Once, on being asked by the Pharisees when the kingdom of God would come, Jesus replied,*
> *'The coming of the kingdom of God is not something that can be observed, nor will people say, 'Here it is,' or 'There it is,' because the kingdom of God is in your midst.'*
>                                          Luke 17:20,21

The Pharisees ask Jesus, 'When's it coming? When will the kingdom of God be here?'

And Jesus says, **It's here now.**

The Pharisees missed it.

Called to keep heaven in mind.

**It's here now.**

If the kingdom of God is in our midst, that means it's not far away. It's right here among us, weaving through life.

We're entwined in glimpses of heaven.

But we often have our eyes shut.

We miss those glimpses.

Called to keep heaven in mind.

**It's here now.**

Where do you glimpse heaven?

Father God
Help me to look at things in the light of heaven.
Amen

We can be like the Pharisees. Looking for something we already have.

Where is God?

God is right here; he's in your midst.

Psalm 139:5: 'You hem me in behind and before, and you lay your hand upon me.'

Where is peace?

Peace is right here; it's in your midst.

Colossians 3:15: 'Let the peace of Christ rule in your hearts, since as members of one body you were called to peace. And be thankful.'

Where is encouragement?

Encouragement is right here; it's in your midst.

Romans 15:5: 'May the God who gives endurance and encouragement give you the same attitude of mind toward each other that Christ Jesus had.'

Where is joy?

Joy is right here; it's in your midst.

John 10:10: 'I have come that they may have life, and have it to the full.'

How does Paul press on? How does he do it?

Keeping going, day after day, can be hard.

> *Not that I have already obtained all this, or have already arrived at my goal, but I press on to take hold of that for which Christ Jesus took hold of me. Brothers and sisters, I do not consider myself yet to have taken hold of it. But one thing I do: forgetting what is behind and straining towards what is ahead, I press on towards the goal to win the prize for which God has called me heavenwards in Christ Jesus.*
>
> Philippians 3:12–14

He learns to forget. Forget the past. And allow the present to be illuminated by the future.

A 'now' focused on heaven.

My facial nerve was damaged in one of my brain surgeries. The nerve doesn't work. I have a half-smile, one side of my face unable to reflect the other.

Over time, I've learned to not think about it. I still don't like it, but it doesn't feature in my thinking so much.

Once, a friend saw an old family photo. There was I, right in the middle of the photo, smiling symmetrically. It was before the damage.

She looked at it, then uttered the words which kick-started my forgetting, or not-remembering, about who I used to be.

'I prefer you now, because that's how I know you.'

I preferred me before. But before was gone. Now was here.

'I prefer you now, because that's how I know you.'

*You have searched me, LORD, and you know me. You know when I sit . . .*

Psalm 139:1,2

The word translated 'sit' here refers to settling, or inhabiting.

He knows the world you inhabit as you sit.

He knows where you'll sit tomorrow.

And the next tomorrow . . .

And he sits with you.

Father God
Help me to truly know that you want me
just as I am.
Amen

After Paul came to know Jesus, he went to join other Jesus-followers in Jerusalem. And they were scared of him.[1]

They didn't believe he really followed Jesus now.

They, too, had to learn to forget.

How do we learn to forget? We train ourselves to remember.

*So from now on we regard no one from a worldly point of view. Though we once regarded Christ in this way, we do so no longer. Therefore, if anyone is in Christ, the new creation has come: the old has gone, the new is here!*
                                                2 Corinthians 5:16,17

Because of what Jesus did on the cross,[2] Paul no longer looked at people from a worldly point of view. He looked at them through heavenwards eyes.

Sometimes, looking at people and keeping heavenwards in mind can be hard. People hurt us. We want to lash out at them, or we harbour resentment. Understandably.

Jesus didn't pretend that we should not acknowledge things like this.

**It will be difficult. But I'm sending you anyway.**

When God made the world, he made people. People in his image.

If God made everyone in his image, the image of God is in everyone.

'The kingdom of God is in your midst.'

As we look around our world today, it can be hard to believe the kingdom of God is among us. There's so much war, hatred, unhappiness, dis-ease, suffering, selfishness, conflict.

But, if we look, we'll see kingdom glimpses. Good things. Foretastes of what's to come when we've travelled heavenwards to heaven itself.

*The wolf will live with the lamb, the leopard will lie down with the goat, the calf and the lion and the yearling together; and a little child will lead them.*

Isaiah 11:6

'We regard no one from a [human] point of view.'
Train yourself to remember not to rewrite those words.
'No one' here includes you. Don't turn it into 'I regard no one except myself from a human point of view'.
The kingdom of God is in the midst of you.
It is.
A kingdom which says, weakness is welcome.
A kingdom which says, 'Come to me [Jesus], all you who are weary and burdened, and I will give you rest.'[3]
**I know you're weighed down. Come despite that. Come because of that.**
**Just come.**
**I welcome you.**

Father God
Help me to be kind to myself.
Amen

In Luke 14, Jesus told a parable:
A man planned a banquet. He sent out invitations and, when the time for the party arrived, he sent his servants to tell the guests to come. 'Everything is ready for you. Please come!' But the guests said no. 'We're not coming.'
They all had excuses.
'I've bought a field I need to see.'

'I've bought some oxen and am just going to try them.'
They bought a field without first seeing it? They bought oxen without first trying them out?
It seems back to front, yet how often do we do the same?
Buy into something – a trend, a way of thinking, a belief – without first checking it out with God?
'Did God really say . . . ?'[4]
'I recently got married!'
Does the company we keep stop us from coming to God?

> *Do not be misled: 'Bad company corrupts good character.'*
> 1 Corinthians 15:33

Getting married isn't wrong! Spending time with people isn't wrong. But we need to be careful we don't put any relationships before our relationship with God.

> *Love the LORD your God with all your heart and with all your soul and with all your strength.*
> Deuteronomy 6:5

Father God
Forgive my excuses.
Amen

The man was furious.
Those he'd invited had turned him down. He told other servants to go out onto the streets and invite anyone they could find. Bad, good, it didn't matter. Invite them anyway.

*Go out quickly into the streets and alleys of the town and*
*bring in the poor, the crippled, the blind and the lame.*

v. 21

So the servants did.
But there was still room.
So the king invited more.

*My flesh and my heart may fail, but God is the strength*
*of my heart and my portion for ever.*

Psalm 73:26

I am not good at sewing, but I do have a cross-stitch picture of this verse. It was made for me by a friend when I
was first diagnosed with my medical condition.
She made it for me because, as I lay in bed, huge tumours
newly discovered in my head, awaiting life-threatening
(as well as potentially life-saving) surgery, my flesh was
failing. And God gave me this verse.
**Your flesh and your heart may fail, but I am the strength**
**of your heart . . .**
My flesh was failing.
My heart, too. I was scared.
In a way, my flesh was making excuses. Why would God
want you? You might as well give up. You're falling apart
anyway. You're useless.
And God breaks in.
**Bring in the poor, the crippled, the blind, the lame.**
**The ones with tumours. The ones without tumours.**

**The tired. The rejected. The weak. The struggling. The ones who don't think I want them. Invite them. Show them they're wrong.**

*Here I am! I stand at the door and knock. If anyone hears my voice and opens the door, I will come in . . .*

Revelation 3:20

Anyone.
**I am the strength of your heart.**
'The kingdom of God is in your midst.'

Father God
The strength of my heart
is you.
Amen

*I press on towards the goal to win the prize for which God has called me heavenwards in Christ Jesus.*

Philippians 3:14

Keep heavenwards in mind.

My 5-year-old nephew started school. One morning, at about 5 a.m., his parents were woken by noises coming from his bedroom. Going to investigate, his dad found him getting dressed. Caleb was putting on his school uniform but, being unable to tell the time yet, he didn't know he was too early.

That day, his mum bought a light with a timer. She plugged it into a socket in Caleb's room, and at bedtime she explained to him that, in the morning, he was not to get dressed until the light came on. The light would tell him when to get dressed. Tell him when to put on his school uniform. Clothes chosen for him by his school. Clothes which showed which school he belonged to.

Get dressed in the light.

Getting dressed in the dark is difficult. Perhaps Caleb would put on the wrong jumper or the wrong socks. Clothes that hadn't been chosen for him, and all because he wasn't getting dressed in the light.

Get dressed in the light.

Jesus said, 'I am the light of the world.'[5]

The light of your world.

Get dressed in the light.

In Ephesians 6, we are told what we, as heavenwards people, should wear. Clothes chosen for us by God.

Put on the belt of truth. Dress yourself in certainty. In refusal to believe lies. Lies whispered in the darkness: 'Did God really say . . .?' Doubt introduced about yourself.

Psalm 25:5: 'Guide me in your truth and teach me, for you are God my Saviour, and my hope is in you all day long.'
Wrap yourself in truth for the journey.
You're called heavenwards.


Put on the breastplate of righteousness. Dress yourself in honourability. In refusal to compromise.
1 Corinthians 16:13: 'Be on your guard; stand firm in the faith; be courageous; be strong.'
Protect yourself with righteousness for the journey.
You're called heavenwards.


Put on shoes of peace. Wherever a day takes you, stand on peace. However stressful your situations are, stand on peace.
John 14:27: 'Peace I leave with you; my peace I give you. I do not give to you as the world gives. Do not let your hearts be troubled and do not be afraid.'
Navigate your way with peace for the journey.
You're called heavenwards.


Pick up the shield of faith. Hold on to God, so you can resist attempts to attack and distract you. As a child, I learned a simple definition of 'faith':
Forsaking All, I Trust Him.
Matthew 8:26: 'He replied, "You of little faith, why are you so afraid?" Then he got up and rebuked the winds and the waves, and it was completely calm.'
Hold your shield in faith for the journey.
You're called heavenwards.

Put on the helmet of salvation. Dress yourself in victory. Victory over your mind. You've been saved from allowing negative thoughts to dominate. Or external influences to rule. Protect your mind.

2 Corinthians 10:5: 'Take captive every thought to make it obedient to Christ.'

Care for yourself by being covered in salvation for the journey. You're called heavenwards.

Pick up the sword of the Spirit. Take God's Word with you. Hold onto it. Memorize it. Make it part of you.

Psalm 119:105: 'Your word is a lamp for my feet, a light on my path.'

Keep your sword close as you journey.

You're called heavenwards.

Father God
Help me live in your light.
Amen

On a flight, people often have two (or more) bags, packed before the journey. One bag to go in the hold, and one to go in the cabin. The cabin bag contains things they might need on the journey: books, pillows, games. Or perhaps essential medications. The airlines have strict cabin bag size rules; if your bag is too big, you don't get to keep it with you on the flight. It goes in the hold.

We need to make sure we keep heavenwards clothes in our cabin bag as we journey. Close by, easy to put on again if they've slipped off a bit. But sometimes, we try to fit extra clothes in our cabin bag.

Belt of falsehood alongside the belt of truth.
Breastplate of self-sufficiency alongside the breastplate of righteousness.
Shoes of worry alongside shoes of peace.
Shield of doubt alongside the shield of faith.
Helmet of defeat alongside the helmet of salvation.
Sword of the world alongside the sword of the Spirit.

Our cabin bag grows, and it can't stay with us. It goes in the hold, at the bottom of the plane. The armour God gave us has been squashed out of reach by the armour we've given ourselves.
And that's not good.
Ephesians 6:11 says, 'Put on the full armour of God.'
Wear it.
Get dressed in the light.

Father God
Help me not to overload my cabin bag.
Amen

*I press on towards the goal to win the prize for which God has called me heavenwards in Christ Jesus.*
Philippians 3:14

Paul clothed himself in determination. He 'pressed on'.
God clothed that determination in heavenwards.

*Once you were not a people, but now you are the people*
*of God; once you had not received mercy, but now you*
*have received mercy.*

1 Peter 2:10

*I saw the kingdom of heaven today.*
*A child told a man in a suit*
*about her day,*
*in all its 3-year-old detail,*
*and he stopped what he was doing,*
*crouched down beside her*
*and listened.*
*I saw the kingdom of heaven today.*
*A teenager with neon hair*
*offered his seat on the bus to a lady*
*five times his age,*
*unplugged his earphones,*
*and listened to her stories from long ago.*
*I saw the kingdom of heaven when she*
*in turn*
*asked for his stories*
*and his mask of cool crumpled*
*and he told her he'd failed his exams*
*and she gave him a hug.*
*I saw the kingdom of heaven today.*
*On a train*
*when a woman smiled at a woman*
*who was holding back tears*
*as commuters glared at her*
*as she wished she could stop her*

*baby's cry*
*and, from that smile, she*
*received strength to smile back*
*and mean it.*
*I saw the kingdom of heaven today.*
*I said my flesh*
*and my heart*
*are failing,*
*and God said*
***I am the strength of your heart,***
***so your heart is strong.***
*And he reminded me*
*I'm pressing heavenwards with*
*the kingdom of God in my midst.*


Father God
Help me to be like Paul.
Pressing on.
Eager to travel the heavenwards journey.
Teach me to learn to forget where I should.
And to remember where I should.
Thank you that you are on this journey with me.
And heaven is ahead.
Amen

## REFLECTION

- Where did you glimpse heaven today?
- In what situation do you need to remind yourself that 'God is in your midst'?
- What do you need to learn to forget?
- What do you pack in your cabin bag for the journey?

## GOD'S CALLING CARD

# Final Bit

*But now, this is what the LORD says – he who created you, Jacob, he who formed you, Israel: 'Do not fear, for I have redeemed you; I have summoned you by name; you are mine.'*

Isaiah 43:1

At the end of the book of Joshua, in chapter 24, Joshua gathers everyone together and, for the final time, he passes on to them what God is saying.

God is reminding the people where they came from.

Right back to Abram being called by God to leave his country and become a nation.

To Moses, leading the people in the desert after God had parted the Red Sea to help them escape Egypt.

And up to the present day, with the people entering the land God had promised them.

Then Joshua passes on some advice himself:

*Now fear the LORD and serve him with all faithfulness. Throw away the gods your ancestors worshipped beyond the River Euphrates and in Egypt, and serve the LORD. But if serving the LORD seems undesirable to you,*

*then choose for yourselves this day whom you will serve,
whether the gods your ancestors served beyond the Euphrates, or the gods of the Amorites, in whose land you
are living. But as for me and my household, we will serve
the LORD.*

vv. 14,15

'Choose for yourself who you will serve. As for me, I will
serve the Lord.'

Some of the last words Joshua spoke.

The people said, 'We will serve him, too!' and so Joshua set
up a stone pillar. A calling card, in a sense. A monument to
remind them of their promise. A promise they'd only made
because Joshua had been there.

But Joshua was going.

And leaving that calling card to remind the people he had
been there.

What calling cards do you leave as you go through life?
Things that say, 'I've been here.'

*But the fruit of the Spirit is love, joy, peace, forbear-
ance, kindness, goodness, faithfulness, gentleness and
self-control.*

Galatians 5:22,23

Maybe you think it's too difficult to leave those calling
cards all the time.

Peace? *But I'm prone to anger.*

Goodness? *But it's not fair that I always have to be the good one.*

Love? *But it's impossible to show love to some of the people I meet.*

> *If anyone is in Christ, the new creation has come: the old has gone, the new is here!*
>
> 2 Corinthians 5:17

The new is here.

> *But now, this is what the* LORD *says – he who created you, Jacob, he who formed you, Israel: 'Do not fear, for I have redeemed you; I have summoned you by name; you are mine.'*
>
> Isaiah 43:1

Instead of 'summoned', the NLT has 'called'.
**I have called you by your name.**
What is your name?
Your name is 'God's special possession'.

> *As you come to him, the living Stone – rejected by humans but chosen by God and precious to him – you also, like living stones, are being built into a spiritual house to be a holy priesthood, offering spiritual sacrifices acceptable to God through Jesus Christ . . . You are a chosen people, a royal priesthood, a holy nation, God's special possession, that you may declare the praises of him who called you out of darkness into his wonderful light.*
>
> 2 Peter 2:4,5,9

Chosen by God.
Belonging to God.
Called out of darkness.
His special possession.

**Dear Special Possession**
**You belong.**
**You are chosen.**
**Every day.**
**I choose you.**
**I wrote your days.**
**Will you express them back to me in praise?**
**Every day, I call you out of darkness.**
**You can be the person I call you to be.**
**Darkness won't win.**
**You're in my light.**
**Will you reflect it back to me in worship?**
**My voice is the one that calls you.**
**You'll know it's me, because**
**I call you by name:**
**'My special possession.'**
**God**

'You write books, don't you?'
'Yes,' I replied.
Five-year-old Josiah leaned towards me.
'I'm writing a book, too.'
We discussed his plot, his characters, his storyline.

I hesitate to say I quizzed my nephew, but perhaps I shouldn't.

I asked him when the book would be finished.

I'm pleased to say, I did not use the word 'deadline'.

'In about a week.'

'Oh, good,' I said. 'Next time I see you, perhaps you can bring the book to show me.'

'Yes,' he nodded. 'I will. And then you can read it to me.'

I could read words he had written.

And I could read them to him.

> *All the days ordained for me were written in your book before one of them came to be.*
>
> Psalm 139:16

As we live our lives, in a sense we are reading what God has written in his book.

When I read Josiah's book back to him, I won't choose the words. I'll read what's written. What I will have a choice over is the expression in my voice as I read.

Will I read in a lively way?

Or monotone?

Or stilted?

Or excited?

Or interested?

Or bored?

Or invested?

I'll have to wait and see, but I'll certainly be excited, interested and invested.

I know I will, because I know and love the little boy who wrote the words.

As we live the days God wrote for us, reading them back to him, how do we read?
Do we try to change the script, or rub it out, or ignore it?
Or do we read back what God has written for us?
What do our lives express?
**Will you speak your love to me?**

> *Do not conform to the pattern of this world, but be transformed by the renewing of your mind. Then you will be able to test and approve what God's will is – his good, pleasing and perfect will.*

Romans 12:2

Do not conform to a world which often says, 'I'm going to drag you down.'
A world which often loses you in a sea of anonymity.
Remember. Renew your mind. Every day.
God wrote about you in his book.
You're not a nobody.
You are called.
By God himself.
Called.
Live called.

> **'Do not fear, for I have redeemed you; I have summoned you by name; you are mine.'**

Isaiah 43:1

# Acknowledgements

Thank you to my sixth form English teacher, for consolidating and sharing my love of words, and for being a constant encouragement.

If this book were a race – which it isn't! – these three would be my pacemakers:
Mum at the starting gun.
AJ in the middle.
Jane at the finish line.
Thank you to each one.

And, as always, thank you to God, who knows me by name. He is the Pacemaker of my life.

# Notes

## Introduction

[1] https://eighteenseventyeight.com/2016/08/11/the-history-of-the-calling-card-2/ (accessed 18.1.19).

## 1 Adam and Eve

[1] Genesis 3:1.
[2] See Genesis 3:5.
[3] Matthew 28:20.
[4] See Genesis 3:10.
[5] Genesis 3:11.
[6] Genesis 3:13.
[7] John 21:22.
[8] See Genesis 3:21.

## 2 Hagar

[1] Genesis 17:15–27.

# 3 Abraham

[1] See Genesis 17.
[2] See Mark 7:31–35.
[3] http://www.greatadventure.carterclan.me.uk/?p=380 (accessed 4.2.19).
[4] See, for example, ESV.
[5] ESV.

# 4 Moses and the Burning Bush

[1] Exodus 3:5.
[2] Exodus 3:6.
[3] Exodus 3:8.
[4] See 2 Corinthians 4:7.
[5] https://www.goodreads.com/quotes/63168-i-can-do-things-you-cannot-you-can-do-things (accessed 18.1.19). But note: there is some doubt that this was quoted by Mother Teresa.
[6] Exodus 3:3.

# 5 Moses Up the Mountain

[1] See Matthew 11:28.

# 6 Moses and the Cloud

[1] See Exodus 24.
[2] See Exodus 3:14.
[3] Verse 29.
[4] Exodus 24:16.
[5] See Genesis 2:2.

## 7 Samuel

1   1 Samuel 3:9.
2   https://nameberry.com/babyname/Eli (accessed 21.1.19).
3   See Matthew 3; John 3.
4   Exodus 33:18.
5   1 Samuel 3:15.
6   1 Samuel 3:18.
7   John 12:28.
8   Job 38:2.

## 8 Israel

1   Story based on Luke 15:11–31.
2   John 8:12.
3   John 19:30.

## 9 Ananias

1   https://www.christianquotes.info/quotes-by-author/hudson-taylor-quotes/#axzz5eeliQpWe (accessed 5.2.19).
2   See Acts 9.
3   An American spiritual, recorded by Laurie London and becoming a hit in the late 1950s. Label: Parlophone. Writers: Robert Lindon and William Henry.
4   See https://www.godupdates.com/story-behind-it-is-well-with-my-soul/ (accessed 5.2.19).
5   2 Corinthians 12:9.
6   John 8:12.

## 10 God

1 Psalm 119:145.
2 Exodus 3:14.
3 https://eighteenseventyeight.com/2016/08/11/the-history-of-the-calling-card-2/ (accessed 22.1.19).
4 See Isaiah 43:4.

## 11 Paul

1 See Acts 9.
2 See 2 Corinthians 5:14.
3 Matthew 11:28.
4 Genesis 3:1.
5 John 8:12.

**Authentic**

We trust you enjoyed reading this book from Authentic. If you want to be informed of any new titles from this author and other releases you can sign up to the Authentic newsletter by scanning below:

Online:
authenticmedia.co.uk

Follow us: